B&T
$7.95

D1531738

NOISE THE NEW MENACE

NOISE THE

NEW MENACE

by Lucy Kavaler

The John Day Company / New York

Wingate College Library

LIBRARY OF CONGRESS CATALOGING IN PUBLICATION DATA
Kavaler, Lucy.
  Noise: the new menace.

  Bibliography: p.
  1. Noise pollution.   I. Title.   3-4-76
TD892.K33 1974   363.6   74-9367
ISBN 0-381-98274-2

1   2   3   4   5   6   7   8   9   10

Copyright © 1975 by Lucy Kavaler

All rights reserved. No part of this book may be reprinted,
or reproduced or utilized in any form or by any electronic,
mechanical or other means, now known or hereafter invented,
including photocopying and recording, or in any information
storage and retrieval system, without permission in writing
from the Publisher. Published simultaneously in Canada by
Fitzhenry and Whiteside Limited, Toronto

Designed by Jack Meserole

Manufactured in the United States of America

Other Books by Lucy Kavaler

FREEZING POINT   *Cold As a Matter of Life and Death*
MUSHROOMS, MOLDS, AND MIRACLES
THE ASTORS   *A Family Chronicle of Pomp and Power*
THE PRIVATE WORLD OF HIGH SOCIETY

FOR YOUNG READERS:

LIFE BATTLES COLD

COLD AGAINST DISEASE

DANGEROUS AIR

THE WONDERS OF FUNGI

THE ARTIFICIAL WORLD AROUND US

THE WONDERS OF ALGAE

THE ASTORS   *An American Legend*

067019

610799

In memory of
Dr. Max Kavaler

ACKNOWLEDGMENTS

My aim in this book is to show the harm that noise pollution does to man and his environment. Noise is affecting man's hearing, his health, his peace of mind, and pleasure. It is also my goal to describe what is being done, and what more can be done to fight the noise menace.

My research, therefore, has covered man's physical and psychological health, animal and plant life and the ecosystem, laws, technological improvements, citizens' actions, the sources of noise, and the state of noise pollution and control abroad. In these investigations I have received help from experts in each field. Many have supplied me with research reports that have not been published or are not generally available.

For information about the state of knowledge about noise today, I should like to thank Dr. Cyril M. Harris, Professor of Electrical Engineering and Architecture, Columbia University.

Assistance for the chapters dealing with the effects of noise, physical or psychological, was given me by Dr. Paul Borsky, Director of Noise Research, School of Public Health, Columbia University; Dr. Thomas Fay, Director, Speech and Hearing Clinic, Columbia-Presbyterian Medical Center; Dr. Joseph Danto, Director of Audiology, City College of New York; Dr. Jerome Lukas, Sensory Sciences Research Center, Stanford Research Institute; Dr. David C. Glass, Professor of Psychology, New York University; Dr. Lester Sontag, retired Director, Fels Research Institute; and Dr. Stephen A. Falk, National Institute of Environmental Health Sciences, U.S. Department of Health, Education and Welfare.

My investigations into the legal approach to noise control were much helped by Dr. Albert E. Rosenthal, Professor of Law, Columbia University; Robert Bennin, Acting Assistant Director of Noise Abatement, New York City; Wendell Blair, National Institute of Safety and Health; Alvin G. Greenwald of Greenwald & Baim, Los Angeles; a detective on the New York City Police Force; and Senator John V. Tunney's office.

Information about aircraft noise, both legal and technological aspects, was given me by Dr. John Powers, Chief Environmental Scientist, Federal Aviation Administration; Nicholas Yost, Deputy Attorney General in Charge of Environmental Unit, Office of the Attorney General of California; and Milton Sherman, Principal Assistant City Attorney, Los Angeles.

The problems of noise in housing were described to me by George E. Winzer, Chief, Urban Noise Abatement Research Program, U.S. Department of Housing and Urban Development.

My research into the effects of noise on animals and plants was assisted by Dr. James Bond, Animal Husbandry Research Division, U.S. Department of Agriculture; Dr. John L. Fletcher, Professor, Memphis State University; Dr. David Van Haverbeke, Research Forester, U. S. Forest Service; and Dr. Pearl Weinberger, Associate Professor, University of Ottawa.

Information about the technology of noise control was given me by Lewis S. Goodfriend, acoustical engineer, Morristown, New Jersey; Gerald Franz, Secretary, Washington, D. C., Chapter, Acoustical Society of America; Dr. James Botsford, Senior Noise Control Engineer, Bethlehem Steel Corporation; Dr. Jerry Tobias, Chief, Communications Processes, FAA Civil Aeromedical Center; as well as spokesmen for a number of companies manufacturing soundproofing materials.

Traffic and transportation noise were discussed with me by Christine K. Helwig, Supervisor, Mamaroneck, New York; William Leasure, National Bureau of Standards; and William H. Close, Chief, Research Division, Office of Noise Abatement, Office of the Secretary of Transportation. Information on snowmobile and motorcycle noise was furnished me by Robin Harrison, Mechanical Engineer, U.S. Department of Agriculture, Forest Service.

For the section on citizens' activities, I received information from Dr. William A. Shurcliff, Citizens League Against the Sonic Boom; Theodore Berland, Citizens Against Noise; John T. French, Quiet Highways; Lloyd Tupling, Sierra Club Washington representative, and members of other Sierra Club groups; George Alderson, Friends of the Earth; Rod Vandivert, Hudson River Valley Council; and Robert Alex Baron.

I should like to thank members of the staff of the Office of Noise Abatement and Control, U. S. Environmental Protection Agency, for their assistance in providing me with information and supplying me with documents and transcripts of testimony presented at those public hearings which I was unable to attend myself.

For the section on noise in Japan, I should like to express my gratitude to the many people who helped to arrange interviews for me with the country's leading noise experts during my visit there. Among others, I spoke with Saburo Matsui, National Environmental Protection Agency; Kuniji Toda, Ministry of Transport; Kutaro Ishino, Civil Aviation Bureau; Takashi Shimodaira, Motor Vehicles

Department; Kazuo Arai, Railway Supervision Bureau; Tomio Mochizuki, Tokyo Metropolitan Research Institute for Environmental Protection; Mieko Baba; Dr. Yasutaka Osada, Institute of Public Health; Shiro Onishi, director of Public Hazards Office, Kyoto City Government; Noboru Nakatsuki, Bureau of Public Health, Osaka City; Hirofumi Nozaki, Osaka City Environment Division; and Takakazu Nakamura, Osaka Prefectural Environmental Pollution Control Center.

My research for this book has been carried out over a period of years and at an early stage I received a great deal of assistance from (positions given are those they held at that time): Brig. Gen. William F. McKee, Administrator, FAA; Raymond Shepanek, Director, FAA Noise Control Staff; Isaac Hoover, FAA Office of Noise Abatement; Dr. Stanley Mohler, Medical Consultant, FAA; Dr. Donald F. Hornig, President Johnson's Science Advisor; Merlin Smelker, U. S. Department of Housing and Urban Development; N. Y. Congressman Theodore Kupferman; Dr. Howard M. Bogard, psychologist; Dr. Julius Buchwald, psychiatrist; Dr. W. Dixon Ward, Director, Hearing Research Laboratory, University of Minnesota; Dr. Wilbur J. Gould, ear specialist, Lenox Hill Hospital, New York; Milton W. Hamilt, executive vice-president, Lenox Hill Hospital; Dr. George Urban, Consultant, U. S. Public Health Service; Dr. Alexander Cohen, U. S. Public Health Service; Herbert Jones, Division of Occupational Health, U. S. Public Health Service; Stannard M. Potter, United Acoustical Consultants of Darien, Connecticut, and Neil Anderson, chairman of New York Task Force on Noise.

I should also like to express my thanks to my agent, Marie Rodell, and as always, to Arthur.

CONTENTS

SHATTERED SILENCE, 1   1

TO SLEEP NO MORE, 7   2

THE ANNOYANCE FACTOR, 18   3

NOISE AND THE INFANT, 30   4

THE SOUND THAT DEAFENS, 36   5

CAN MAN ADAPT TO NOISE? 53   6

THE ANIMAL MODEL, 61   7

OF WILDLIFE, PLANTS, AND THE BALANCE OF NATURE, 68   8

A LAW AGAINST IT, 77   9

JAPAN: THE WORST NOISE, THE BEST LAWS, 93 10

MAKING THE MACHINE RUN QUIETLY, 110 11

PROTECTING THE HOME, 122 12

AN IMMENSITY OF SOUND, 131 13

AND FROM THE AIR, 144 14

THE "WHISPER" PLANES, 157 15

THE PEOPLE AGAINST NOISE, 166 16

BIBLIOGRAPHY, 181

INDEX, 199

NOISE THE NEW MENACE

SHATTERED SILENCE 1

IN THE POND *at the center of the marsh the frogs call to their mates. Many different species occupy the same pool and the land around it and a loud chorus rises. Nearby birds sing lustily and small animals scurry about rustling leaves and padding on the earth. Yet the ears of the frog are so finely attuned that any female can distinguish the call of the bull of her own species from the rest. Each species of frog broadcasts its mating call on a particular frequency band and at a particular pulse rate.*

Sound and sex are so intermingled in the animal world that the sow copulates most vigorously when she hears the signal of her male partner.

Creatures, regardless of their position on the evolutionary ladder, pass auditory information. At the approach of danger one bee warns others by emitting short bursts of sound. Sea gulls call to one another where food is to be found. Even the earthworm signals in a series of dots and dashes.

The bat flies unhesitatingly through the darkness of the cave. It finds its way around obstacles, escapes predators, and locates prey by sending out ultrasonic sound waves and listening for the echo. The porpoise similarly depends on the echo to guide it through the murky underwater world. It can detect an object, living or inanimate, that is no more than 0.2 millimeter in diameter.

And what of man? His hearing is so brutally assaulted by the technological noises of the world that he has lost the sensitivity other creatures possess. He makes up for the dulling of his sense by a series of devices and substitutions. The voice is raised to a shout. Alarm signals are made more strident. Radios and television sets are played at higher volume and musical instruments are amplified. Electronic radar and sonar equipment help man to locate obstacles with the precision of the bat.

Something is lost that no amount of skill in electronic design, substitution, and amplification can ever find again. The pleasant sounds of life are drowned out.

"I am thinking of a night I spent at a beautiful lake in New Hampshire," said a witness at a public hearing of the United States Environmental Protection Agency. "Then a motor boat came along, and that ended it."

Peace and quiet, the cliché phrase, stands for a dream—impossible to achieve without some sacrifice. Where can one go to be free of the noise made by the products of modern industry? Where can one go to find silence? There are still oases of quiet for the very rich or for those who will resolutely hold out against the lure of good income, interesting job, varied companions, and perhaps fame in the urban centers. Others make do with a few hours in quiet surroundings obtained at the cost of long train rides or traffic jams morning and evening, or flee to a weekend or vacation retreat. Each respite makes the return harder.

With every passing year, the oases grow fewer. The scope of the forest ranger has been cut down with the trees. The individual farmer tilling his small plot of ground is an anachronism in an age of huge mechanized farm industries. A climber who reached the peak of Mount Rainier, 14,410 feet above sea level, could hear diesel trucks from a distant highway.

Far to the north near the Arctic Circle the Eskimo villages are closed in each winter by snow and darkness. Until recently, only the shouts of children, the barking of the dogs, the occasional howl of a wolf broke the stillness. No highways cut through the miles of ice surrounding the most isolated Eskimo communities in northern Alaska. Yet the roar of engine noise now fills the Arctic night. The Eskimo leaves his home, climbs into his snowmobile, starts the motor, and drives off to go hunting. A little later his teenage son sets out for the Eskimo Cafe or Polar Bear Theater in the family's second snowmobile. Only a few years ago the father journeyed slowly by dogsled and the son went as far as his snowshoes would take him.

No one would want the Eskimos to return to snowshoes and dogsleds as the only means of conveyance; their lives, still hard by temperate zone standards, are richer and easier now. In remote frigid regions the snowmobile is the rescue vehicle, bringing searchers to the person lost in a snowstorm or a doctor to the suddenly stricken. But in most parts of the world, the snowmobile is chiefly a new toy. As recently as 1960 only a few hundred were in use. By now some two million shatter the silence of the last open spaces of the United States and Canada with a noise like that of a screaming chain saw. Manufacturers are quieting machines in response to legislative requirements, but the best level hoped for, and this not for some years, would be equivalent to average city traffic noise. And the snowmobile goes through regions formerly undisturbed, havens for those who love solitude, and the habitat of hibernating animals.

The snowmobile deserves attention because it is typical of recent technological advances, bringing some good to the standard of living and some harm to the environment. Like other machines of modern times, it carries noise ever farther. In temperate zones new highways take engine noise and tire screech to millions who thought that leaving the city would solve their noise problem. About 96,000 miles of roads go through the suburbs. The building of needed housing has blasted city living with the din from jackhammers, riveters, drills, and air compressors. The jet airplane that makes travel a pleasure for the traveler makes staying at home a burden for countless people on the ground.

The noise laboratory of the University of Tennessee was for some time occupying space in the football stadium. In the spring of 1972 construction began on an addition to the building. The scientists soon were unable to work, their experiments on the effects of excessive sound drowned out by the construction noise.

"It's rather strange when a noise study laboratory can't function because of the noise," said the director.

The situation was quite different when the monkey house in a large city zoo was being enlarged. Hearing the construction crew beginning to drill, the zoo director came out and insisted that they stop: "The apes won't stand for it!" A change to quieter building methods was hastily made.

Noise has degraded the quality of life. Yet of all forms of pollution, it has received the smallest amount of attention. Where air pollution can kill and water pollution cause disease, noise acts so insidiously that its effects are hard to pin down. Air pollution produces something that can be seen and smelled—fumes, smog, haze, dust on the tabletop, grime on hands and hair. Water pollution makes rivers, bays, and estuaries murky, trash-filled, and foul-smelling. But noise is here and is gone. Who can even say what it is? The standard definition is "unwanted sound," but unwanted by whom and when?

A hotel guest complained to the manager about the noise of the piano playing in the next suite, goes an often-told story. "But that is Artur Rubinstein practicing for his concert," was the reply. The guest invited several friends to come to her room where they could have the privilege of listening to the great artist.

Clearly, one man's joyful sound is another's noise.

The noise vocabulary is unfamiliar. Anyone can grasp the facts of air pollution as measured by the number of parts per million of a pollutant. But noise is figured in decibels (abbreviated dB), a unit not in everyday usage.

Environmentalists frequently are asked, "What are you using now instead of the decibel?" by people certain that a measurement more readily understood by the general public must have been devised since their schooldays.

The basic unit bears the name of Alexander Graham Bell, and zero decibel is arbitrarily set as the softest sound the ear can hear. A one-decibel sound will move the eardrum a distance one-tenth the diameter of a hydrogen atom. The loudest that is bearable is 10 million million times greater than zero decibel.

The sound of breathing as one sits quietly reading is 10 decibels. No one measured the sound level in the cork-lined room where Marcel Proust shut out the world, but it may have come close to the 20 to 30 decibels of the wilderness area where the silence is broken only by the rustle of leaves or the cry of a bird or small animal. Office noise gets to 60 decibels or higher, and it takes the 80-decibel-ring of the alarm clock to get the worker to that office on time. Rush-hour traffic can reach 92 decibels. Aside from the thunderclap of 120 decibels, a sound level louder than 100 hardly ever occurs in nature. To make such noise commonplace requires the efforts of man. A jet plane at takeoff equals the thunderclap, as does the din within a discotheque. Measurements are obtained with an electronic device, the sound-level meter.

"The most annoying sound known to man is produced when a saucepan is scraped by a knife," wrote a British noise expert.

A violin's music at the same decibel level is far less irritating. The difference lies in the frequency, which gives each tone its quality and pitch. This changes according to the distance the sound wave travels through the air to complete its cycle. The farther it goes, the lower the frequency, and the fewer the number of cycles occurring in a second. The low frequencies can be felt in the body. There is a buzzing in the ears, sensations in the chest and abdomen. High-frequency sound, which has a short wavelength, is dissipated more rapidly than low. Even so, the high-frequency noises are most shattering to the nerves, as they are the more shrill.

People will adjust to some noises, but not to others. A city dweller slept undisturbed by the traffic passing beneath his window. It was familiar and carried no threat. Then he moved to the country, and awakened repeatedly at the rustle of leaves to consider its significance. The initial reaction to an unfamiliar noise is alarm.

In the early years of the twentieth century, a Society for the Suppression of Unnecessary Noise was formed: "To the sensitive, noise, even amidst spacious surroundings, is disturbing, in uncomfortable quarters, it is torture."

The group urged "the removal of one of the greatest banes of city life."

In the years since then, the torture of noise has increased, not abated. Yet the spirit of that manifesto was never more in tune with the thinking of large numbers of people than it is today. Those who seek quiet are beginning to triumph.

A Paris nightclub, Crazy Horse Saloon, has been ordered to soundproof the hall where striptease shows are performed to the background of rock music.

A neighbor had complained to the police. "I heard everything, but saw nothing," he declared.

And after the noise was stilled: "Justice is done."

TO SLEEP NO MORE 2

"HOW MUCH SLEEP, *I ask you, can one get in lodgings here? . . . The wagons thundering past through these narrow twisting streets, the oaths of draymen caught in a traffic jam— these alone would suffice to jolt the doziest sea-cow of an emperor into permanent wakefulness."*

More than 1,800 years have passed since Roman satirical poet Juvenal composed these lines. Substitute a few words and they speak for us today.

To describe noise as maddening is to use a cliché, but like many, it holds considerable truth. While noise of itself will not drive a sane person to insanity, it is often a goad to irrational behavior and violence.

A few years ago four boys were at play in front of a building in the Bronx, New York. Suddenly a gun appeared in a second-floor window and shots rang out. One of the boys, the son of a political figure, fell dead. The police assumed an opponent of the father was involved in the murder until the killer explained that he was a night worker and had to sleep during the day. The noise made by the youngsters kept him awake and he lost control of himself.

"There are people who are prone to shoot others. There are many sad, deranged people in this city," said a New York City police lieutenant. "Noise could aggravate them."

Something else might trigger senseless action in the unstable, he added, but noise is the most unnecessary of annoyances. "Some individuals get terribly irritated by noise and become ready to quarrel with anyone who happens to be present. As the second person responds in kind, the pressure between them mounts until one might hit the other."

A writer, normally mild-mannered, swears it to be true that he became so furious at the late night noise made by a woman upstairs that he bought a gun and started target practice. All at once it dawned on him that what he was contemplating was murder, so he moved away instead.

In pre-Nazi days Franz Schoenberner was editor of *Simplicissimus,* a German satirical publication. After Hitler came to power, Schoenberner, an anti-Nazi, fled to France where he was for a time in an internment camp. Eventually he managed to make his way to New York and settled there. One day he insisted that a neighbor turn down the radio. The neighbor in a rage attacked Mr. Schoenberner and injured him so severely that he had to use a wheelchair.

Some years ago, a sewer was being built in Kansas City. A doctor complained to the city administration about the jackhammer banging away for hours of the day beneath his window. Nothing was done to stop it. One day he put on a tuxedo, slipped a carnation in the buttonhole, took a homburg hat and kid gloves, and went out to the work project. He walked up to the hammer and swung at it with gloved fists. The only result was a fine of $50 for disturbing the peace and $2 for damage to the jackhammer.

The doctor might have decided to move away; prison inmates

have no such option. Reformers are pinpointing noise as a source of psychological trauma that must be removed from the prison system. During an inquiry that led to the closing of the Manhattan House of Detention, the Tombs prison, a tape made inside the prison was played for members of the Board of Correction. The director of the city's Bureau of Noise Abatement asked those present to try to talk with one another while this was going on. They quickly gave up the effort. The only way to communicate was by shouting. The necessity for shouting, together with the uncomfortably high background noise level, contributes to the emotional unrest of the inmates. A psychiatrist testified to his belief that two of every five persons incarcerated in the prison were disturbed or mentally ill.

"They yell. I yell back. We have all developed the habit of shouting even when there are no planes passing overhead," a teacher from Barnes Junior High School in East Boston told an Environmental Protection Agency public hearing. "There is a dramatic increase in fights . . . a rash of brawls. When you ask a youngster why, he'll say 'I feel nervous and jumpy.' "

A spot check of faculties of a number of schools in the area brought these results: 34 of 35 who responded had to stop teaching during overflights; 33 said they lost appreciable amounts of teaching time; 33 declared that noise-induced abnormal behavior had increased greatly recently.

"We're quite convinced our barbiturate problem is at least in part due to a desire for quiet," commented other witnesses at the hearing.

An otherwise peaceful man got out of his car one day and struck another driver. The offense, he realized later, was unbelievably trivial. He had been cut out of a line of traffic. Similar scenes, or at the very least threats of bodily harm, are played out every day on the streets of any city. The bad temper of taxi and bus drivers is legendary. The steady bombardment of noise added to the effect of the exhaust fumes drives many beyond endurance.

The struggle to block out unwanted noise causes tensions to build. One of the first things to go is a sense of humor. A husband and wife will suddenly explode in anger at one another over a minor incident; a parent will strike a child for "nothing." That minor incident or nothing may really be excessive noise. A mother in Osaka, Japan, first threw her child into a well and then jumped in herself, seeking sanctuary from the noise of jets at nearby Itami International Airport. Suffering from Ménière's disease, a disturbance of the inner ear, she found the din a final unbearable insult.

Two neighbors in a suburban community have not spoken to one another for several years. The feud was caused by a high-fidelity system blaring on a Sunday morning.

When interviewing property owners near Kennedy Airport for a National Academy of Sciences study, Dr. Albert E. Rosenthal, Columbia University law professor, was particularly impressed by the attractive quality of an upper-middle-class community. But it had a major drawback: its location in the center of the noise impact area. A year later he heard that violence and hostility among the residents had erupted.

"I wonder whether the excessive reactions might not be in part a result of the jangled nerves of people living right in the flight path of jet planes landing and taking off many times a day," said Dr. Rosenthal. "Noise may have permanent effects on the social fabric of life, changing social interrelationships."

The magnitude of the problem becomes apparent when one considers that loud urban traffic noise can be heard both by day and at night in the homes of at least four million people, and probably twelve, while four to seven million are bothered by noisy aircraft, and another one to three million live too close for comfort to construction sites.

Most people try to escape all this at least once a year and go to a peaceful place for a vacation. The belief that rest and quiet are needed for mental health has considerable longevity. Mental hospitals are usually in secluded areas, away from a city.

Noise is particularly threatening to the person who is psychotic or approaching that state. In an effort to determine how much it means to such individuals, psychiatrists reviewed reports of admissions to a British mental hospital over a two-year period. They quickly saw that the number of patients from a residential area close to noisy Heathrow Airport was larger than from quieter communities. But upon closer scrutiny, it appeared that only certain people were affected. The increase occurred among women aged 45 or more, and single, whether spinsters, widows, or divorcées. They are most vulnerable to the assault of noise. Many come to the end of a working life, lacking the companionship and financial support a mate provides others.

Psychotic individuals find noise deeply troubling. The schizophrenic responds violently, as has been shown by biochemical tests performed after tapes of 90 decibel sounds were played. Levels of hormone in the urine were as high as those that appear during episodes of extreme aggressiveness. The schizophrenic does not get used to noise, even to a limited extent. He reacts no matter how often he hears it. The same inability to grow accustomed to noise is characteristic of brain-damaged children, the hyperkinetic, and those suffering from a form of senile dementia.

Fears and anxieties of the mentally ill are increased, a further indication of the probable contribution of noise to their state. A California psychiatrist has described a hospitalized woman who insisted that the footsteps of nurses going down the hall at night were those of a messenger of death coming for her. Others become completely preocuppied with a certain noise or overreact to the barking of a dog, ring of the telephone, or distant conversation. A young patient became tense and excessively excited whenever anyone around him whistled. In time it was brought out that he associated whistling with his father.

While the psychotic patient's reaction was extreme, the experience is universal. Just as the taste of a "madeleine" reminded Proust's hero of his childhood, a sound can release a flood of remembrances. Some years ago Dr. Wilder Penfield of McGill University, Canada, performed an experiment in which he painlessly stimulated parts of the cortex of the brain of patients who were under local anesthesia. Asked to report what they thought, most recalled experiences of the past. The voices, words spoken, and background sounds were very vivid parts of a memory. A noise, whether loud or barely perceived, may, therefore, set off the recollection of a painful experience.

Tiredness, insomnia, difficulties in relationships at home, irritability, and gradual reductions in sexual drive and desire were some other responses to noise exposure made by people with no psychiatric history. These were civilian maintenance workers at Wright Field who for long periods were subjected to frequent sound levels of 140 decibels.

After two years at the field, five of 10 men showed some impairment of the higher brain functions. They did not react as efficiently as formerly to stimuli entering via the sense of touch. Two of the men had severe neurotic symptoms, and two had mild ones. Maintenance personnel on the aircraft carrier, *Wasp,* were affected in similar ways.

In another study, brain waves of Italian weavers were found to present patterns very similar to those of people known to have personality disorders. Weaving is one of the noisiest of industries, and all had been working for long periods. Their reflexes were faster than normal, evidence of a highly nervous state.

On the other hand, the desire to do nothing can be a reaction to noise exposure. Sixteen rhesus monkeys from the Wisconsin Regional Primate Research Center were forced by students to listen to one, then three, then five hours of hard rock music blared over a loudspeaker. Later they had another five hours with recordings of noise from such machines as power saws and pneumatic hammers. The sound level was held at 100 decibels. As the hours passed, the monkeys lay down or sat quietly and stared vacantly off into space. This was far from typical behavior for these normally lively animals.

Does this experiment tell anything about man? While Wisconsin's Professor Robert E. Bowman, chairman of the psychology department, warned against "extrapolating to humans" too literally, similar human behavior does not seem illogical. Hours of rock music or industrial noise bring a sense of weariness. The exhaustion that follows a day at work is in part due to noise.

Then comes the night. During World War II United States Navy pilots flew over the Solomon Islands of the South Pacific tossing empty beer bottles out of the hatches. These made frantic high-pitched whistles as they plummeted from the planes, interrupting the sleep of the enemy below, and tiring him before the next day's fighting.

A New York State legislative committee on jet noise was told that paranoid delusions, hallucinations, suicidal, and homicidal impulses were possible consequences of major sleep loss.

The harm done by noise invading the sleeper's world is more subtle and insidious. He must rouse to determine whether the sound represents danger or a prosaic situation requiring his conscious activity. The child's call brings his mother to his side; the alarm clock tells the worker to get up and go to his job; the shout of "fire" sends the family out of the building. This warning system is repeatedly and unnecessarily called into play by an automobile horn, an unmuffled car racing by, a helicopter, ambulance siren, a radio turned on next door, or the garbage trucks arriving for a predawn pickup.

Wingate College Library

Individual variations are great. One person wakes if a faucet starts to drip in a downstairs bathroom, while another sleeps through an electric guitar playing in the next room, or a fire alarm. Most sleepers will awake at a noise above 70 decibels. At 50 decibels about half will either awake or shift out of deep to a light, troubled sleep, and sensitive people will be disturbed by a sound as moderate as 40 to 50 decibels.

If a plane flies over a house, which of the residents will be most likely to wake up? The grandmother, grandfather, mother, and father, and in that order; the small children will usually be undisturbed. To determine whether this observation is true, a test was carried out at Stanford Research Institute by Dr. Jerome S. Lukas. Regular aircraft flyovers and sonic booms were simulated, and the adult and child participants were not told whether they would hear any noises on a specific night, or if so, how many. When awakened, they were to press a switch by the bed. The children, aged five to eight, were without exception remarkably insensitive to the noise and slept through. The middle-aged were awakened by about 18 percent of the noise intrusions, and the old people by 32 percent. Among those of the same age, women are more sensitive.

A noise need not be intense to produce wakefulness. Most will awaken at a sound they have prepared themselves for before going to bed. This may be the soft closing of the door by the teenager coming home from a date. The man on the 6 A.M. shift will arouse at the first ring of the alarm clock, while his wife beside him may sleep on. Psychiatrists in World War II England noted that during the worst of the bombardment mothers would sleep peacefully in crowded, noisy shelters. But while undisturbed by the loud crying of other people's children, a mother would awaken when her own baby started to cry.

Some background noises induce sleep rather than restlessness, and a number of "sleep shops" sell recordings of lapping waves or gentle rain to be played at bedside. The peaceful breathing of children in the next room, the snores of a spouse are reassuring and help the sleeper to rest.

On the other hand, some sounds harmless in the daytime produce anxiety at night. To a person in a half-waking state, the banging of a door may suggest that someone is breaking in, the child's murmur is taken to mean that he is in pain or ill. The sense of uneasiness lasts after the noise has been identified.

A sound may not be loud enough—or personally meaningful enough—to bring the sleeper to full wakefulness, but yet be sufficient to shake him from one level of sleep to another. During the night each sleeper passes through various stages, recognizable by means of characteristic brain waves recorded on an electroencephalogram. The speed and frequency of these brain waves differ from one stage to the other. One of the stages can be identified just by looking carefully at the closed eyes. A series of rapid horizontal eye movements can be detected through the eyelids. This REM stage is the one at which dreams take place.

"The most harmful noises are those that invade your dreams, because dreaming is necessary for mental health," stated psychologist Howard M. Bogard, who served on the Mayor of New York City's Task Force on Noise Control. "Most people have four to six dreams a night. If the dream is interrupted by a jet plane, fire engine, or noisy neighbor, the person will dream twice as much the next night. But if he is interrupted again and again, he will become emotionally upset. And it does not take long; a few nights are enough."

A group of paid subjects took part in an experiment on dreams. Each time one of them began to dream, as revealed by his rapid eye movements, he was awakened. Many dropped out of the test after only two or three days, being too agitated to continue.

Sometimes a sound will not tear a person out of his dream, but will enter and change it into a nightmare.

The noise that does not awaken the sleeper may have a lasting effect on him, nonetheless. A number of different sounds were played during the night to volunteers at Stanford. The sleepers moved back and forth from deeper to lighter stages. The next morning they did not remember having been disturbed and could not describe any of the noises. Still, they complained of feeling tired.

"The 'I'm not up to snuff' feeling is almost impossible to measure," said Dr. Lukas. "We gave out a questionnaire asking whether a lack of sleep affected work on the following day. Most replied that it had relatively little effect. This fits in nicely with some of the more rigid laboratory studies. In these when volunteers were deprived of sleep, no difference in performance on the job the next day was noted —until they were down to three hours of sleep a night. People have the tendency to compensate for a deficiency and force themselves to apply more energy when they are tired. But no one has tried to investigate what would happen to their work if sleep were inadequate for very long periods."

That has been done to two young male chimpanzees at the Aerospace Medical Division of Holloman Air Force Base. For 30 nights the monkeys' sleep was troubled by 24 impulsive noises. In the days following they performed the tasks they had been trained to do more poorly than previously. Although they did in time get somewhat accustomed to the noisy night, they never returned to the prenoise performance standard. It is reasonable to assume that man would be at the very least as troubled as the chimpanzee.

The deprivation of sleep and of dreams, the destruction of a sense of peace, intrusion into privacy, interruption of conversation, disturbance of activities, added to the grating and annoying nature of certain sounds and the impossibility of escape are even harder for the sick, than the healthy, to endure. As the Society for the Suppression of Unnecessary Noise wrote in the early 1900s, "unnecessary noise first wrecks health and then is chief torment of illness."

When the sound level in the recovery room of a hospital was high, reported a trade journal of nursing in 1968, post-operative patients required more medication to control their pain than when it was quieter. Although the study was not complete enough to satisfy all scientific criteria, it confirms the long-held view that a sickroom should be quiet.

Suffering a hangover, the late comedian W. C. Fields complained about the din of the Alka-Seltzer fizzing in the glass.

In 1309 the Knights Hospitalers of St. John of Jerusalem came to the island of Rhodes in the Aegean Sea. The hospital that they built has windows facing an open inner court. To the street, it presents an almost solid wall of thick stones. In this way the Knights protected the sick from the annoyance of noise coming from the busy town of Rhodes.

THE ANNOYANCE FACTOR 3

" R E D U C T I O N *of annoyance, or the pursuit of happiness, is not necessarily an ignoble end.* "

That such an obvious statement need be made at all—let alone defended—seems an absurdity to any layman. But as spoken by British noise expert Donald E. Broadbent, it reveals the problem faced by the researcher today.

Once the scientist moves from experiments showing hearing loss to be caused by long-term exposure to excessive noise, he enters a never-never land where one set of studies proves noise to do considerable damage of a certain kind, and another set shows that it does less or none at all.

Asked repeatedly to "prove" that noise is harmful, Dr. Cyril M. Harris, Columbia University noise expert, takes Dr. Broadbent's aphorism one step farther: "To me, annoyance is a sufficient cause for noise control."

The capacity of noise to annoy is equaled by few other assaults on the senses. The scratch of chalk or a fingernail across a blackboard is so repellent that to hear it makes a shudder run down the spine.

"The widespread dislike of certain sounds needs no more explanation than the taste of the rat (and of many humans) for saccharin," pointed out Dr. Broadbent, who is with the Applied Psychology Research Unit, Cambridge.

In order to show what sound means to people, decibel scales have been worked out that go beyond measuring loudness alone. As people hear best in the 1,000 to 6,000 cycles per second frequency range, the A scale gives particular weight to those speeds. The annoyance factor has been added to create the Perceived Noise in Decibels (PNdB) scale. It takes as a starting point 40 decibels and a frequency of 1,000 cycles per second, as softer sounds are not likely to annoy anyone, and this counts as one PNdB. As a refinement on this scale, acoustical experts have added an important aspect of annoyance—how long the noise lasts. A sophisticated scale, the Effective Perceived Noise in Decibels (EPNdB) scale includes time as part of the subjective reaction.

Relationships between the various scales have been figured. The barking of a dog, found to be 85 dBA, and 89 in PNdB units, was only 81 EPNdB, because the bark did not last long enough to be very annoying.

No measurement, however, can account for individual reactions. What annoys one person may please another. Some are more noise sensitive than others. Even the same individual does not invariably react in the identical manner. Daily and monthly internal rhythms affect response.

"In a noisy environment, about one-fourth of the people are not disturbed no matter how loud the noise, and about a tenth are disturbed no matter how faint the noise," according to a study sponsored by the American Society of Engineering Education and the National Aeronautics and Space Administration.

Some put the proportion of imperturbables at one-third.

"If you could change just one thing in the environment, what would it be?" "Noise," answered 12 percent of 4,000 residents in a 15-mile radius of London's Heathrow Airport. The individuals being questioned were not told that the purpose of the survey was to determine their reaction to noise. Yet when asked to select aspects of community living they disliked particularly, nearly a quarter spontaneously picked out aircraft, traffic, and other noise. When asked whether and why they ever felt like moving away, 17 percent of those sampled replied that they would like to move away from the noise.

A pet dog's barking makes the owner feel safe; the neighbor's animal is a menace. The crying of a child next door bothered 7 percent of a British group questioned: only 5 percent complained when their own babies were sounding forth.

Americans will not tolerate interruption of television and radio, public opinion surveys reveal. Next in terms of annoyance comes drowning out of face-to-face or telephone conversation. But even when it does not mask an activity requiring hearing, noise intrusion into outdoor recreation or indoor relaxation is bitterly resented.

What home today seems like a castle? The number of units in apartment houses has increased; the space between suburban and even rural houses has decreased. Walls, roofs, ceilings, and floors have become too pitifully thin to provide protection from the sound of toilets flushing, telephones ringing, radios playing, dogs barking. Strangers perforce listen in to quarrels over money or infidelity, to the cries of the baby with colic, to the teasing of younger brothers and sisters. Many Americans today know more about their neighbors than they would like and fear that their neighbors know too much about them. Some admit to conducting private conversations in whispers.

There are those who go so far as to welcome the traffic noise from outside. "At least it is impersonal," remarked a tenant in a large modern apartment building. "And it drowns out the voices and activities of the people next door."

"The loss of privacy in our homes is destructive of family life," psychologist Bogard has said. "A husband and wife cannot even quarrel or talk freely together. No room in the house offers a sense of seclusion."

This side-effect of shoddy construction is seldom recognized. "In considering the stresses of urban life, I think what is bothering people most is the breakdown of delivery of basic services," said Dr. David C. Glass, professor of psychology at New York University. "For example, a few years ago if your neighbor were too noisy, you could have your walls insulated and windows fixed. Today you cannot find someone to do the job quickly and when you bring in a workman, he will do it badly and overcharge."

In addition, noise itself induces the very psychological reaction that does much to prevent its control.

"There is a phenomenon of helplessness," said Dr. Glass. "Anxiety results from the recognition that one is helpless to do anything about the noise. Each person concludes that he is being intimidated by forces beyond his control. He is powerless and at the mercy of others."

This feeling of utter helplessness contributes to the often extreme reaction to airplane noise. "It goes beyond the mere fact that the jet plane is so loud that it breaks into conversation or sleep and frightens small children. The adult who hears it subconsciously thinks 'I'm so small and the intruder is so big and all powerful. What can I do?' This leads to feelings of impotence and frustration," commented Dr. Bogard.

These feelings can be distressingly accurate. At a public hearing on noise held by the Environmental Protection Agency an official whose duties included operating an airport was told that noise was unbearable in a nearby low-income community occupied by members of a single ethnic group. Clearly surprised that anyone would listen to complaints from this source, he remarked: "Some people stand noise much better than you or I."

An odd aftereffect of noise disturbance was detected during an experiment conducted by Dr. Glass. Volunteers were required to play a variation of the old children's game of tracing over all the lines of a diagram without lifting the pencil or retracing any lines. They could try as many times as they wished. Two of the diagrams were impossible to complete correctly, but the students were not told that. They did these repeatedly, becoming increasingly exasperated. When the background noise was soft and regular, the subjects kept on trying no matter how often they failed. But when their concentration was interrupted with loud unpredictable noises, they gave up early. The exposure to this kind of noise left them with a lower tolerance for frustration.

Under what circumstances do people stand noise best? The undergraduate volunteers at New York University were to proofread manuscripts while noise was played at random intervals. Some of the students were given a button to push whenever they wished to stop the noise; the others had none. The mean percentage of errors in proofreading made by those who could control the noise was 28.22 percent, while those without the control button had a rate of 42.44 percent. Moving one step farther out into the world, it can be seen that the Federal Aviation Administration holds the control button for aircraft, the builder the control button for the air compressor.

Having someone to complain to is nearly as important as being able to press the button yourself. Some of the New York University volunteers were paired. One had a control button and the other was told he could signal his request that this be pushed. He did not know whether his partner would respond. Even so, students who could ask for help made fewer proofreading errors than did others who saw no way of escaping from the noise.

"This is the same effect as would come from feeling that you have access to City Hall," commented Dr. Glass.

But the palliative effect achieved by establishing a "city hall" or noise control agency with a procedure for complaints wears off when no action follows. Many individuals living close to airports or heavily traveled highways have come to believe in the malevolence of those in charge.

At an Environmental Protection Agency hearing, witnesses referred repeatedly to the "lack of sensitivity" of agencies in charge of airports. "We will put your complaint on record" tended to be the response . . . the only response.

Those residents of housing developments near airports who are convinced that the aircraft companies are guilty of building noisy planes for profit are far more troubled by the noise than those who think the companies are doing as well as they can and mean to do better.

The attitude toward the source of noise is a major factor in determining the degree of annoyance. As a major function of noise is to serve as warning, many are alarmed by it. "We live under constant fear," said a resident of East Boston near Logan airport. "We always think that there might be an accident."

Others do not associate aircraft noise with the danger of a crash and endure it more easily.

Those who suffer noise love company. The worker who believes he is exposed to more noise than others reacts most strongly. If he thinks he has less noise around him he is not so bothered by it. And this is true even when the noise level is higher than he would normally accept.

The way people feel about their jobs also affects the response to noise. A worker was told his functions were particularly important to the production record of the entire factory: his morale remained high even when he was placed in the noisiest part of the plant. He did better than others working in moderate noise but with the view that their tasks were not of overriding importance.

The power of suggestion is so great that when a group of workers was told that noise would make performance on the job deteriorate, this happened. A second group was told that people work more efficiently when background noise covers interruptions. The results were exactly what one would expect.

The foreman who sneers at the idea that workers will be less efficient in noise "is probably adopting a sound strategy," remarked Dr. Broadbent, but this applies to work output only. Should management ignore noise, hearing loss is more likely to result than increased efficiency.

In an effort to improve worker output, the management of a factory initiated a noise-control program and greatly reduced the background levels. Production increased promptly. Later there was an expansion program and the additional equipment brought in pushed the noise level back to its original highs. Nonetheless, the output continued to be good. The workers were responding in both situations to the interest being shown by the management. Noise had little to do with the result. As production statistics influence management's decision on noise-control investment, this is frustrating for those seeking to prove the need for quieting industry.

Efficiency is a good indicator of the effects of noise on man, wrote Dr. Broadbent. "A person may say he is not affected by conditions and yet not work well, or say he hates them, but is doing well."

Some workers bitterly resent the requirement of earplugs, but show the greatest improvement in output when using them.

The individual working in noisy surroundings may become tense, irritable, and tired, but this does not necessarily destroy his efficiency. That is particularly true of those tasks requiring simple repetition. When a job is more complex, efficiency may drop off at first, but eventually pick up again. People tend to overcompensate and work harder than usual against the disturbance of noise. On a short-term basis, this may actually increase the quality of attention paid to a task and raise output.

Noise may mask distractions that would otherwise deflect a person from his work. A clanking or hammering machine makes it impossible to hear the conversations of other workers, the footsteps of the girls going by, the birds singing outside. Background music or the sound of an air conditioner can thus have a useful masking effect. A "white" noise is sometimes provided by engineers to achieve the same result in an even less distracting way.

"White noise is all sounds," said Lewis S. Goodfriend, who heads his own acoustical engineering firm in Morristown, New Jersey. "If you take all the sounds you hear at once in a busy part of a city—from the lowest to the highest—and mix them in at once, you will make white noise. Any tuning fork will respond to it. This is random noise."

White noise can occur in nature. A waterfall produces it. A low-pitched rumble, a roar, a rushing sound like wind, a high-pitched rustle of leaves—all these together are the sound of a waterfall.

In order to give privacy, white noise can be produced electronically and played through loudspeakers, usually placed out of sight above a grid or acoustical tile ceiling. In open office space such planned noise can cover private conversation; for much the same reason, a number of psychiatrists have installed the device.

The story is told of a titled gentleman, a lover of note some decades ago, who often took a party cruising on his yacht. He ordered that the ice machine be kept on all night. The sound covered up the footsteps, tapping, whispering, doors opening and closing, so that guests could slip undetected into one cabin or another.

White noise is used in some offices that are exceptionally quiet, for silence is distracting as well as revealing. Yet white noise, called "acoustical perfume" by engineers, annoys some people. They object to any sound imposed on them by others. Such individuals must object strongly to the sound forced on them by noisy machinery.

Regardless of whether noise is imposed or selected voluntarily, it is particularly hard to learn a new task in a noisy environment. This was proven by an experiment in which volunteers were handed a series of items and told to use them to build equipment of a type they knew little about. Eight of 24 individuals working in quiet surroundings were able to complete the model in less than quarter of an hour. Only three of 24 working in noise did as well. But when the work was repeated day after day, by the fifth, the difference between the two groups had become insignificant.

Clock watching—with a clock that made double jumps at random intervals—was the subject of a test carried out at the Aeromedical Laboratory of Wright-Patterson Air Force Base. Each double jump was to be noted. Whether working against a background noise of 79 or of 112 decibels, the volunteers were equally accurate. Then they were given three jumping clocks to watch, and the noise level was raised to 114 decibels. This time the number of misses was greater in noise. Individuals can manage to keep track of changes in the movement of just one device. To follow more requires a flexibility of attention, and this is the capacity affected by noise.

The implications are clear for managers of automated factories where one person must monitor control panels with indicators detailing events over the entire plant. Some can increase the intensity of attention to the point where they can overcome the adverse affects of noise; others cannot.

Participants in a government study took a standardized personality questionnaire, the Minnesota Multiphasic Inventory, to see if noise were more unsettling to certain personality types. Extroverts and individuals with neurotic tendencies were below average in vigilance tasks in a high-noise background.

A steady sound level of 90 decibels or lower will not affect the performance of the average person, but sudden or intermittent bursts, even though softer, can cause work to deteriorate. High-pitched noise is not only the most disagreeable to listen to, but also the most disturbing to concentration.

An unexpected noise, whether a shout, gong, siren, motorcycle, or backfire, demands interpretation. If a person is engaged in a project where a temporary lapse of attention is permissible, then the end result will not be altered. But in certain jobs even a momentary break in concentration can be disastrous. The numbers of the dial change constantly, the assembly line moves past, the object goes out of radar range. Not only are errors caused and information irrevocably lost, but accidents can occur.

The person doing two tasks at the same time is likely to perform more poorly in noise, because the brain is overloaded by the mass of stimuli.

"It becomes more and more necessary for the brain to do something to prevent this from interfering with appropriate goal-directed behavior—with the focusing of attention," neurobiologist Robert G. Grenell of the University of Maryland School of Medicine explained to the Environmental Protection Agency.

The brain must cut out some of the extraneous, unwanted stimuli, possibly by functioning beyond its normal capacity. Such activation could lead to fatigue, aggression, and other side-effects. It may also explain the anesthetic effect of noise that has been called into play by a good number of dentists. Perhaps the auditory stimuli take over to some extent those brain cells that must process the impulse of pain and transmit it to higher nerve centers.

The way it works in dentistry is that the patient is given earphones and music is played. As soon as the dental work begins to hurt, he presses a switch and changes the music to noise. The greater the pain, the more the intensity of the noise is increased. Of the several thousand dentists who used sound, one-third reported that patients were completely relieved, another third saw patients partially, but significantly helped, and the balance found the noise of no benefit. When the noise did work, the patient was in much better condition following the dental work or surgery than if he had received local or general anesthesia. But as pain relief depends in large part on whether the patient believes he is being helped, the suggestion of the dentist, not the noise, may be responsible.

Under most other circumstances the confusion produced by noise is annoying rather than anesthetizing. Sound without meaning or relevance for the individual—and that is true of aircraft or traffic noise—is particularly aggravating. The intrusion seems purposeless. The degree of annoyance is greatly lessened when a person can be made to see, or to believe, that there is a purpose.

Residents of a community near a military airport complained repeatedly about the noise. They were then furnished with propaganda material that stressed how important the Air Force is to the national defense. It also said that plans to lessen the noise had been made. The number of complaints fell abruptly.

"The reduction was equivalent to the effect that would have been obtained by lowering the noise levels by six decibels or so," reported Dr. Paul Borsky, director of Noise Research at Columbia University's School of Public Health. He did not suggest this as a substitute for lowering the noise levels by six decibels or so—and reducing the complaints for reasons actual rather than ephemeral.

Rich people are more likely to complain about noise than are poor, older rather than younger, and well educated than poorly educated. The others may suffer as much, but are more inclined to suffer in silence.

Subjective reaction can transform even a clearly unpleasant noise into one that is enjoyable. Columbia law professor Rosenthal was visiting Yosemite National Park one summer when military planes broke the sound barrier. The resulting sonic boom bounced off the mountains on each side, so that the boom reverberated. He found the noise, louder than thunder, to be intolerable. But another tourist looked about cheerfully and remarked: "Listen; they're showing us how the echo works."

The tourist, although oblivious of it, faces the same risk as the knowledgeable law professor. Noise represents a danger to all states of life, the Environmental Protection Agency was told—from the embryo to the aged.

NOISE AND THE INFANT 4

A THOUSAND YEARS AGO expectant mothers in China attended prenatal clinics to seek aid in achieving a state of tranquility. This, it was thought, would be passed on to the infants. Over the centuries there have been periods when pregnant women were encouraged to look at the paintings of Raphael and Leonardo da Vinci and listen to Bach and Brahms in order to influence their unborn children favorably. At other times this view has been held up to scorn. Today some scientists are investigating whether noise experienced during fetal life could affect the child's later development.

"We have been able to demonstrate a statistical relationship between quick movement or activity during the fetal period and social apprehension at two and a half years," reported Dr. Lester W. Sontag, retired director of the Fels Research Institute, Ohio.

The fetus responds to noise with a substantial increase in body movement and heart rate. In Dr. Sontag's studies children with this recognized prenatal background were reluctant to leave home to go to nursery school. They were worried that the other children would push them around. In nursery school, while they did take part in the organized activities, they were careful to avoid fights. And oddly enough, the relationship between fetal activity and apprehension was found to be greater by far in boys than in girls.

The effect of noise on the fetus was documented in 1925 by German scientist A. Peiper. With reports appearing in the literature, physicians turned their attention to the phenomenon familiar to any woman who has borne children. Whenever music is played, the fetus becomes more active. In a concert hall the kicking and activity reach a peak when the audience applauds.

To determine the nature of the response, Dr. Sontag and his colleagues asked each of 17 pregnant women volunteers to select a favorite piece of music. Electrodes were attached to the abdomen and the music was played. Heart rates of both mother and fetus, measured on an electrocardiogram, rose as the song was heard.

For many years it was believed that the infant in the womb would respond to sound only indirectly—with his mother as the medium. Slight hormonal changes took place in the mother's body as she listened to the music or noise, and the hormones released crossed the placenta. Noise experts continued to agree with the view expressed in 1895 by the German researcher W. Preyer: The fetus cannot hear sound, because its middle ear has not developed sufficiently.

This theory was overturned by a variety of experiments. When a wooden disk on the mother's abdomen was lightly struck with a noisy electric doorbell clapper, almost all infants responded with a speeded heart rate and increased activity. Both reactions were so rapid, coming within four to five seconds that it was taken as evidence of "direct fetal perception of the sound."

Thus, some noises come to the unborn child directly through his own senses, others through his mother's reaction.

The studies about the psychological effects of noise during embryonic life are not conclusive. Yet, like so much of noise research, they carry a disturbing suggestion.

"Animal experiments have shown that conditions existing during pregnancy can be related to deviations in behavior in adult life," said Dr. Sontag. When infant animals are exposed to noise and then observed in adulthood, they are found to be more emotional. And males are more affected than females. "But there is so much in human life—it is so complex and hard to study—that no one really knows the effects of fetal stresses. Still, the proposition that there are carryovers appears logical."

Even in the absence of documented research, he considers it advisable for pregnant women to guard themselves against noise. "Any expectant mother should get out of New York," Dr. Sontag commented wryly, conceding that this would seldom be feasible. "Just as other excessively strenuous or stressful things are given up during pregnancy, noise should be considered as important, too. The stress of excess noise has been grossly neglected."

It is a danger, even if fetuses experiencing noise regularly become conditioned to it, as was implied by a study of babies in Itami City, near an international airport in Japan. During the peak daytime hours airplanes fly over the city at four- to six-minute intervals. Most infants whose mothers had spent the first five months of pregnancy in Itami City were able to sleep soundly despite aircraft noise, observed Drs. Y. Ando and H. Hattori of Kobe University. About 13 percent of them cried during overflights. But those children whose mothers had moved to the vicinity of the airport at the end of pregnancy or just after childbirth were very easily disturbed. Half of them cried when the planes went past, while only 9 to 16 percent slept soundly.

Drs. Ando and Hattori think that their findings indicate "the possibility of the evolution of humans to adapt to ever-increasing environmental noise."

Such evolution is not necessarily desirable.

"The organism may change so that it can cope with the environment, but it pays a price. In an evolutionary sense, to adapt to one environment reduces the ability to cope with other environments," stated Dr. Bruce Welsh, of the Friends Medical Scientific Research Institute.

Certain rat studies have offered hints that noise during fetal life may affect the ability of the young animal to learn. Female rats of a strain known to be noise sensitive were kept in an enclosure with an electric bell which was rung loudly twice a day from the fifth through the eighteenth days of pregnancy. The rats born of these pregnancies began a maze-learning test when they were 80 days old. The same test was taken by other rats born to mothers living in comparative silence. Those rodents which had been subjected in fetal life to the electric bell took longer to find their way through the maze than did the others.

Moving from embryonic life to childhood, Sheldon Cohen and Michael Smith of New York University investigated whether noise during this period affected adult ability to perform tasks well. A group of infant rats was exposed for 31 days to continuous noise of 80 to 90 decibels. A second group heard the same noise, but at intervals, and a third was reared with only moderate background sounds. Seven weeks later all were tested. In order to avoid a shock, the rat had to discriminate between signals delivered through a speaker. Those animals exposed to intermittent sound during infancy had the poorest success in escaping the shock. Noises that come irregularly are more annoying than those that are continuous. Thus, the rat would strive mightily to condition himself not to hear such sounds, and might in time become generally inattentive to all noises.

Human children brought up in extremely noisy places become inattentive to sound and its meaning and may be handicapped in their ability to read, write, and speak well. One investigator, C. P.

Deutsch, wrote in the *Merrill-Palmer Quarterly of Behavior and Development* in 1964 of tests made of first-, third-, and fifth-grade children from a noisy slum area. They displayed both poor ability in discriminating sounds and poor reading skills. Comparable tests of children from quiet and more affluent neighborhoods should be made to reveal whether the significant factor was noise or the deprivations of poverty.

Regardless of whether noise affects intelligent performance, the nineteenth-century German philosopher Arthur Schopenhauer had no doubts that it affected intelligent people: "I have long held the opinion that the amount of noise which anyone can bear undisturbed stands in inverse proportion to his mental capacity, and may therefore be regarded as a pretty fair measure of it. . . . Noise is a torture to all intellectual people."

Schopenhauer was an intellectual snob. Who can fail to see that noise is a torture to everyone, regardless of intellectual level?

The effects of that torture on sexual and reproductive function is easier to prove than are alterations in learning ability, at least in animals. Sound stimulated the genital organs, but inhibited reproductive function of rats studied at the Hebrew University in Jerusalem. The male rats ejaculated, but sperm did not fertilize their mates. The rats copulated, and only nine out of 50 efforts resulted in pregnancy, compared to 40 out of 50, which is typical. The females had prolonged or persistent oestrus and enlarged ovaries. Nonetheless, they were less fertile and gave birth to smaller litters than rats which had not been forced to listen to noise.

About half of another group of rats exposed to noise for six minutes of each hour of each day of pregnancy lost their litters. Those that did carry to term gave birth to a disproportionately large number of babies with developmental abnormalities.

Oddly enough, other rats responded to noise with reductions in the size of their sex organs. The result again was infertility.

Whether sex organs got too small or too large for effective function appeared to depend on the type of noise experience. Brief exposure is believed to inhibit release by the pituitary gland of gonadotrophins, chemicals that otherwise stimulate the gonads. This lack would keep down the size of the sex organs. Intermittent or prolonged sound, on the other hand, seemed to stimulate the release of these substances excessively.

Lack of communication between laboratory worker and animal makes it hard to determine whether this over- or under-stimulation affects the desire for sex. The disturbing suggestion has been made that man's sexual drive is reduced by prolonged exposure to extremely loud noise. Loss of libido in a group of people living under conditions of intense noise was described in a report in the *Medical Journal of Australia.* A similar United States study was made of workers at Wright Field. Again, those questioned spoke of a slackening of interest in sex. (Few empirical observations of human behavior in noisy surroundings bear this out.)

The very derivation of the word points to the broad range of damage noise can do. The word "noise" has a strange but peculiarly apt origin. It comes, by a long line of linguistic descent, from the Sanskrit "nau" to the Greek "naus," meaning ship, to the Greek "nausia" to the Latin "nausea" to the Old French "noise," meaning a quarrel or brawl, to Middle and then to modern English.

The second edition of the Webster *New International Dictionary* referred to an "obscure change in meaning" from the Latin "nausea" to the Old French "noise." To us today, the change does not seem so obscure. Noise can as easily produce psychological as physical upset.

THE SOUND THAT 5
DEAFENS

"NATURE *has given man two ears but only one tongue that we may hear twice as much as we speak*" *was the teaching of the Greek Stoic philosopher Epictetus.*

More than 300,000 individual tones can be heard by the healthy human ear. The only part that is seen, the outer ear or shell, has far less to do with hearing than the minuscule structures hidden deep within. There lies an organ only 34 millimeters long, which is the main portion of the hearing mechanism. It is so fragile that it can collapse under the onslaught of noise.

What then is lost? The f, s, th, ch, and sh parts of the spoken word, the song of the bird, the lilting melody of the violin—these are the tones that go first. The person can still hear, but the world is less beautiful to him. Most hearing losses due to noise come so slowly and imperceptibly that for a long time the victim does not even know he has been hurt. The husband who seems not to be listening, the friend who never remembers what was told him, the child who is absent-minded at school. He may not be able to hear what has been said.

Puccini's opera *Tosca* was given one summer's night in the meadow of a city park. The music critic of the morning newspaper devoted most of his review to the difficulty of hearing the melodies over the sound of the airplanes. The soprano was lucky, he commented; her major aria was fitted in between flights.

Many people would not hear the music perfectly, even in a concert hall. Hearing loss is the most common physical disability in the United States today. About 16 million Americans have impaired hearing, including but not limited to those with noise-induced loss. The Deafness Research Foundation, New York, uses a higher figure —one of ten Americans, or some 21 million. The loss most often is greatest in the left ear, for reasons as yet undetermined. The deafened person is not necessarily freed from the disturbance of noise. Background sounds make a hum and roar in which music and words are lost.

As a deaf speaker said at a meeting of the Acoustical Society of America, deafness means living "with a problem that has the power to shut you out so completely that life can become pointless unless you are fortunate enough to experience sensitivity."

Noise is not the only factor responsible for hearing loss, but it may very well be the only one that could be controlled with relative ease. Congenital defects account for a good number of cases of deafness; infections are often responsible, and blows on head or ear may be damaging. Most important, time itself takes its toll of all the senses. When hearing was tested in an old folks' home, 159 of the 181 residents could not understand the spoken word unless it were 40 decibels louder than is normal.

The young adult can hear frequencies from about 20 to 20,000 cycles per second, with the most important for speech lying between 500 and 2,000. Instead of cycles per second, acoustical experts prefer the term Hertz (abbreviated Hz) from the name of nineteenth-century German physicist Heinrich Hertz. After the age of 60 the ear's sensitivity has diminished so that the typical listener fails to hear sounds higher than 10,000 or 12,000 Hz. Neither infrasound, with a frequency of 20 Hz or less, nor ultrasound, at the other end of the range, above 20,000 Hz, can be heard.

A sound level louder than 75 dBA is dangerous if heard five days a week over a typical 40-year career. That is lower than the limit allowed by law for an eight-hour day for workers in industry. The first hint that hearing is being damaged is tinnitus, a ringing in the ears. This goes away and is apt to be ignored, while year by year hearing acuity declines.

Hearing is most keen at ages 12 and 13, but it does not stay so for long. Audiometer tests of Tennessee students gave the sobering information that while only 3.8 percent of sixth-grade children had some degree of hearing loss, 11 percent of the ninth-graders did, and 30.2 percent of the freshmen in college. The last figure seemed implausibly high to Dr. David M. Lipscomb, director of Audiology Clinical Services at the University of Tennessee, so he decided to repeat the study with the next class of incoming freshman. Instead of obtaining the lower figure he had hoped for, this time hearing losses were measured in 60.7 percent. Many of the deficiencies were for sounds at seldom-used frequencies, but even for those used in normal speech the hearing was below expectations for this age.

A larger proportion of children from East Boston schools do poorly on hearing tests than do those attending schools in other areas. The reason? "On one day, the worst I admit, there were ten jets passing overhead in a period of ten minutes," explained a junior high school teacher.

All this sound mercilessly batters the ear. Two of the smallest muscles of the body, the tensor tympani and stapedius, are the guardians of the inner ear. They are located within the middle ear and when sound levels pass 80 decibels or so, they contract and reduce the impact on the inner ear. The contraction is reflex, although a few exceptional people are capable of controlling it at will. If the noise continues at an unchanged level for long, the muscles relax. A change in tone, however, will again stimulate the contraction. In some individuals hearing loss is associated with a weakening of this aural reflex. But even when the muscles are strong, they cannot protect the inner ear, the cochlea, against violent noise attack. Then, too, they do not function equally well at all frequencies. Nor do they function equally well for both sexes.

Scientific study is proving what every woman knows. She hears better than a man does. Women turn down the television set volume and hear what the neighbors are quarreling about, while men make the television louder and miss the point of the argument next door. By the age of 11, a difference in hearing between the sexes was noted by Dr. Lipscomb. Three times as many boys as girls had some hearing loss by ninth grade. At every age the female reveals her auditory advantage. Severe hearing loss is present in 7 percent of men in the late sixties and seventies against 4.7 percent of their female contemporaries.

The difference has in the past been attributed wholly to social and economic causes. Boys play with firecrackers, shoot, ride motorcycles, and drive unmuffled cars more often than girls do. Men are the more likely to go hunting, run power mowers, fly planes, work in the noisiest parts of noisy industries. But according to investigations performed by Dr. W. Dixon Ward of the University of Minnesota's Hearing Research Institute, environment alone is not the key: women really are different from men in their hearing mechanisms. They are less troubled than are men by low-pitched noises like roars and rumbles, and can more easily follow high tones, even when there is background sound.

Dr. Ward has explained both of these differences in terms of the middle-ear muscles which contract to reduce the effect of loud, low-frequency noise. This reflex, animal experiments indicate, also improves the transmission of higher frequencies. Women evidently have more efficient middle-ear muscles than do men.

Once through the outer and middle ear, sound waves enter the snail-shaped cochlea and reach the minute organ of Corti, lined with thousands upon thousands of tiny hair cells. These hair cells pass the sound waves along to the auditory nerve. If noise is loud enough, the organ of Corti can vibrate with such violence that it is torn apart. More often, the hairs simply wear out. When hair cells cease to transmit the sound waves to the nerve, irreversible deafness results.

In 1890 a deaf metalworker failed to hear the approach of a train, walked in front of it, and was killed. A physician made a study of the dead man's ears and discovered changes in the organ of Corti. Hair cells at the beginning of the spiral had been lost. The doctor asked the worker's associates about the kinds of sounds he had been unable to hear and was able to pinpoint the deafness in the high-frequency range. Since then one test after the other has shown that the human organ is more easily damaged by high- than by low-frequency sound, because of amplification by the external ear. A sound of 4,000 Hz will be increased by as much as 18 decibels. A larger number of hairs transmit low- than high-frequency sounds. Thus, one-fifth of those cells can be destroyed with no effect on hearing sensitivity. The same amount of loss in the hairs carrying high-frequency sound produces about a 40-decibel hearing loss.

Loud noise causes the blood flow to decrease, cutting off oxygen to the organ of Corti. At the same time the metabolism of the cell is stimulated, so that it needs more, rather than less, oxygen.

Any noise of 120 decibels produces physical discomfort, as well as danger to the ear, and a 140-decibel sound is acutely painful. Occasionally, but fortunately rarely, a single very loud noise may cause permanent hearing loss. One spring during a fraternity "War" at the University of California, a student lifted his arm to throw a firecracker at the "enemy" fraternity house. The firecracker exploded when not more than 15 inches away from his right ear. The young man never again heard perfectly with that ear.

Such explosive noise could damage the outer and middle ear, which are not affected by the exposure to relatively consistent sound that harms the inner ear. A blast may rupture the eardrum or dislodge the bone. As these outer parts of the ear collect and conduct sound pressure to the inner ear, this is a conductive hearing loss.

An evening in an indoor shooting gallery where noise reverberates off the walls and back into the ear can be extremely damaging. The shots at their peaks reach decibel levels of 140 to 165.

"When I give a hearing test, I can recognize a skeet shooter by his hearing loss," a medical consultant to the Federal Aviation Administration has commented.

After getting off an airplane, most travelers cannot hear perfectly for some minutes or hours. When the construction crew that was drilling on the street goes home for the night, the residents of the nearby houses still must increase the volume of television or radio. After the train has pulled out, a companion's voice remains inaudible. This kind of temporary deafness is commonplace.

Audiometer tests will reveal a loss when taken immediately after a person has walked past a jackhammer or stood near the path of a plane at takeoff. As the level at which sound becomes audible to the individual rises, this is a temporary threshold shift. Should the noise be repeated often enough, then the temporary may shift to permanent.

A series of beeps leads pilots to the proper flight path on foggy nights. In the past, beeps were sent out continuously on a single frequency. Pilots complained that they could hear the beeps at first, but then lost them. The men had become deafened to that frequency. When the sound frequency is changed every few minutes, pilots can continue to hear and bring their planes down in safety.

Firemen, policemen, and ambulance drivers can be deafened,

ironically enough, by the noise they themselves are making. Two fire engines with sirens blaring approached a cross street. Neither reduced speed nor prepared to give way until the other vehicle came into view. A crash was narrowly averted that time; drivers are not invariably so lucky.

"I always go down a one-way street the wrong way," commented an ambulance driver. "That way I know people will see me, even if they do not hear me."

Just as changing the frequency of the beep helps to bring in the pilot, shifts in frequencies of the siren can refresh the fatigued ears of pedestrians and firemen alike. The newer sirens have a two-tone horn with a time interval between them and can be heard at a level 10 to 15 decibels lower than is needed by a siren screaming continuously. The sound is not pleasant, but the warning is effective and does not endanger hearing.

"The ear is more tolerant for interrupted noise signals, as it can rest in the quiet periods," stated Alexander Cohen, chief for the National Noise Study, National Institute for Occupational Safety and Health.

Test subjects were exposed to noise peaks of 103 dBA and allowed to rest at a reduced level of 77 dBA. Others relaxed to sound turned down to 40 dBA. Fewer threshold shifts occurred in those enjoying the truly quiet periods.

Noise breaks are essential to the person whose days are spent amidst unrelenting sound.

"It is generally assumed that the worker in the noisy industry has all the rest of the time when he is not at work to recover. But this is not true," said Columbia's Paul Borsky.

He drives home from work to the sound of engines, tires screeching, and horns blowing. Should he need to take a subway, he stands on the platform while the express train rushes into or past the station making, on the average, a 101-decibel blast of sound. If he happens to use the 86th Street station of New York City's Independent subway, the noise he hears can be as high as 114 dBA. Once he gets into the car, things are little better. For more than half of his ride, the level will be greater than 85 dBA, and peaks can reach 109. The Independent is the noisiest of the lines because it runs on a concrete roadbed. The Flushing IRT (Interboro Rapid Transit) has a special kind of noise hazard: As a train rounds the turns, the wheels rub against the rails with a scream that is louder than an automobile horn at three feet.

"The transit authorities say that the average subway noise is below the level the government sets for industrial workers. But it is different for a person to be paid for being exposed to noise than to be asked to pay for it himself," remarked Dr. Joseph Danto, director of Audiology at City College in New York.

New York City's Environmental Protection Administrator was so appalled by the findings of a 1973 subway noise study that he gave warning in a *New York Times* interview that a mere 20 minutes on the subway would affect the average person's hearing for some 40 minutes afterwards and that 25 to 30 years of daily subway riding could lead to permanent loss.

Any New Yorker whose job depends on keen hearing has learned the truth of that warning; a ride on the subway will put him out of working condition for an hour or so. A piano tuner wears earplugs when traveling to a job. "Otherwise," he declared, "I arrive unable to detect many nuances of sound."

Traveling above, instead of beneath, the earth, is also a noisy experience. Cabin noise in a cruising jet plane ranges from 79 to 88 dBA, according to the location, and during landing and takeoff rises by 12 decibels, but for periods of a minute at a time only. The danger is greater for the plane personnel than for passengers, and many crew members have some degree of hearing loss.

A wealthy businessman took pride in his possession of a helicopter that flew him over the multitudes trapped in traffic jams on the ground. It was a status symbol to him, not a threat to his hearing. Yet the sound level within a helicopter is in the 90-to-100 decibel range, representing a real hazard to those who fly often.

How loud is too loud? If just two minutes of listening to a certain noise leaves you with a marked temporary hearing loss (10 to 20 decibels), avoid it. This is recognized as the danger point.

The person who rejects the noise of airplane, subway, and factory to take a job in the woods is not necessarily escaping from noise and its risks. The lumberman on a chainsaw hears 116 dBA when cutting wood, and 91 when the saw is idling. While the difference between these two levels looks small, it is not, because decibels are logarithmic units. As such, they cannot be combined with simple arithmetic, but instead must be multiplied by 10 again and again. Thus, 10 decibels is 10 times as loud as one decibel, and 20 decibels is 100 times as loud, and 40 decibels is 10,000 times as loud. When the amount of sound is doubled and a second electric guitar or jackhammer joins the first, the total noise level rises by three decibels. Two 80-decibel alarm clocks give out 83 decibels. Take one away; reducing noise by three decibels cuts it in half.

While trying to relax in the living room, millions are forced to hear the multiplying decibels of sound produced by jet planes passing overhead at the same time that traffic is roaring down the highway, sirens are blaring, and drills pounding at excavations in the streets.

Some will react to years of this noise with hearing loss, but others who sit in the same living room are uninjured. While the ear of one individual does not seem very different from that of another, the response to the identical degree of noise may be totally unlike. During World War II hearing losses of some magnitude were noted in a number of soldiers after a day on the firing range. The hearing of others was not permanently injured after weeks of gunfire.

Individual variatons are such that one person who spends a single day in a place where noise levels are 100 decibels or higher may have no loss at all, while a second may have a temporary loss as great as 40 decibels. Records of 6,000 men taken over a long working career showed startling differences after exposure to the same type of noise: one-tenth had suffered a permanent loss of 35 to 50 decibels, another 10 percent showed a decline of only 5 decibels, and the balance fell between the two extremes.

It has long been known that some ears are "weak" and some "strong." An article, "Practical Observations on the Pathology and Treatment of Deafness," appeared in the British medical journal, *Lancet,* in 1830, with the suggestion that there must be some original imperfection of the ear in those who become deaf. There was a solution: Deafness should be treated "with decisive bleeding at its first coming on."

Since then otologists have tried to prevent "its first coming on" by performing a test to identify the susceptible. Individuals are exposed to varying levels of noise and then checked with an audiometer for the degree and duration of temporary hearing loss. While logical in concept, this test has not worked as well as was hoped. Some people have one weak and one strong ear. In addition, the same individual may display a variety of threshold shifts on different days. Better tests are being sought. Still, the present test does help to pick out the most vulnerable, the individuals who should avoid jobs in noisy industries.

Noise was not recognized as a health hazard to industrial workers until quite recently. No lesson was learned from the case of the metalworker killed by the train in 1890. The first study of industrial hearing loss was made in 1930 when a British group investigated the hearing of blacksmiths and found damage. Even so, both in Britain and in the United States, the effects of noise continued to be taken very casually by the noise producers for many years thereafter.

Tests were made in the 1950s of prisoners working in the federal penitentiaries at Lewisburg, Leavenworth, Atlanta, and Terre Haute. Noise levels in these prison industries varied from 75 to 110 decibels. Hearing loss, some of it permanent, developed after only three months. At the end of two years the loss amounted to 71 decibels for convicts working at cotton weaving and 79 decibels for those in the furniture factory mill, while the threshold shift for those assigned to the shoemakers' bench was 9.5 decibels. The deficits were greatest in the 3,000, 4,000, and 6,000 cycles per second frequencies. As the main speech frequencies are 500, 1,000, and 2,000 cps, the deafness was not apparent to the men for some time.

Publication of such reports by the U.S. Public Health Service did not lead to the widespread initiation of industrial noise-control programs. The manager of a too noisy factory is now required by law to provide ear protectors and encourage their use, yet workers remain reluctant to use them.

"Unless it is made mandatory, people just do not wear earplugs. They will not worry about something that might happen years from now," remarked Dr. James Botsford, senior noise control engineer of the Bethlehem Steel Corporation.

One category of ear protector, the earmuff, has the advantage of being so conspicuous that a foreman can see whether it is being worn. But this very advantage is a drawback as well. Workers do not like the appearance. Those who wear them are the subject of jokes by those who do not. Complaints are made that the muffs are hot, cause headaches, and ruin hairstyles. The earmuffs consist of cups, lined with sponge foam or some other acoustic material, fitted over the ears. An inexpensive device, they reduce sound by about 30 to 35 decibels.

The other category consists of the plug placed within the ear. Dozens of styles are available. "Our data show that for about 90 percent of people the cheapest kinds work about as well as the most expensive. The custom-fitted appear no better than standard plugs," said Dr. Jerry Tobias of the Federal Aviation Administration's Civil Aeromedical Institute in Oklahoma City. "There is a psychological matter, though," he added. "People who are given custom-fitted earplugs are more likely to wear them. They view the giving of such plugs as an indication of concern by employers."

Despite the ready availability of plugs and muffs, many people cling to the inefficient way of keeping out noise by putting cotton in the ears. The practice has had considerable longevity, because cotton is in every home.

The most bizarre ear protection was described in a query to the health column of a newspaper. The writer told of a young man working all day in noisy surroundings. He wore flashlight bulbs as ear plugs. Was this advisable?

That story, more sad than funny, indicates how little many people know about ear protection.

"A man who takes pride in his work could stay in a lumber mill indefinitely without harm to his ears. Only the psychologically unstable person would claim his hearing had been damaged."

Was this statement made in Dickensian times? Not at all. It was said only a few years ago to Dr. Hayes A. Newby, head of the division of hearing science at the University of Maryland, when he addressed a lumbermen's group in California. His concern for noise-induced hearing loss was viewed as absurd. Employees in the mills did not wear ear protectors, realizing that they would be marked men if they did.

"Child labor in its heyday was not considered an iniquitous practice by parents or employer. In fresh guise, this attitude continues to represent itself, this time with regard to noise" was a charge made at a British Symposium on the Control of Noise in 1962.

That same year when 700 British companies were polled on noise protection by the Industrial Welfare Society, only 55 replied. Six firms had carried out noise surveys; three had extensive noise-reduction programs, and two performed audiometer tests.

How great is the influence of industry on hearing loss? Some idea can be obtained by observing people living remote from the noises of technology. Some years ago an American ear specialist, Dr. Samuel Rosen, visited the southeast Sudan and tested the hearing of members of the Mabaan tribe.

"Except for the bleat of a goat and other sounds of nature, the Mabaan live in a dramatically quiet, almost silent atmosphere," he said.

Their hearing from ages 10 to 70 was significantly more acute than that of Americans. The comparison between Mabaan and American is not exact, because not only life-style, but also heredity and constitution are very different. Nonetheless, the evidence cannot be dismissed; it points directly to the major role played by technological noise.

Assaults on hearing in a modern industrialized society come on all sides; some are unexpected. A number of antibiotics, quinine, and some other commonly used medications can have the side-effect of increasing sensitivity to noise. The louder the noise, the greater this reaction, reported Dr. Stephen A. Falk, National Institute of Environmental Health Sciences. In most cases the loss of hearing is temporary, lasting until therapy ends. Even aspirin when taken in very large doses can cause a ringing in the ears, and a temporary hearing loss.

Guinea pigs were given daily doses of the antibiotic kanamycin for five weeks without any damage to hearing. Others received no drug but were kept in an incubator with noise levels of 68 to 72 decibels at a frequency predominantly of 125 Hz. They, too, were uninjured. But when guinea pigs received kanamycin while being held in the noisy incubator, then there was hair loss in the organ of Corti.

Whether this finding can apply to human infant as well as to guinea pig is uncertain, but Dr. Falk urged further investigation. Incubators in many premature nurseries have noise of 75 decibels at frequencies below 500 Hz. This would be safe under most conditions, but not necessarily here.

"Levels of noise which are in themselves benign cause damage in the presence of known ototoxic drugs."

Animal experiments suggest that noise presents a greater danger to infants than to adults. A sound level that is safe for older persons may be too high for babies.

On the other hand, repeated episodes of drug and noise combinations, Dr. Falk suggested, might contribute to the hearing loss in the elderly.

While it is tempting to blame all excessive sound on outside sources—industry, transportation, construction—many people bring noise on themselves by choice. The motorcycle, home workshop tools, shotgun, all produce levels that can be hazardous to hearing, particularly to ears damaged by the day's work. Drivers relieve the tedium and increase the risk of accident and hearing loss by playing car radios and tape recorders. Trail bikes run at well above the 80 dBA mark, often reaching 100.

When snowmobile owners were informally interviewed by the Forest Service, they cheerfully described spending four hours— "though a six-hour ride is not unusual"—on the machine on any weekend or vacation day. In addition, they remarked that they often would "play" for an hour or two after work.

Children play, too, with toys just as dangerous to their hearing. Toys that whirr, bang, or pop are presented as gifts. Children often pretend that they are desperate characters, and cap pistols remain popular from one generation to the next. In terms of noise, they are an exact copy of the real gun. A cap pistol providing a bang of up to 138 decibels is allowed on the market with no restrictions. A manufacturer may sell pistols producing 138–158 decibels of sound, provided he puts on a warning label and agrees to devise ways of bringing sound of his future models down to the still intolerable 138 decibel level.

Some toy advertisements actually stress the noise aspect as a part of the fun. This is an approach that should serve as a warning rather than a lure.

One of the greatest of all noise hazards is seized voluntarily and with joy. Rock music is a deafening force equal to or greater than any produced by the industrialists so bitterly attacked as polluters by the young. Rock bands playing with standard amplifiers and loudspeakers give forth a decibel level of 120. They can do better than that with the most modern amplifying equipment. A group of Australians who listened to rock bands once or twice a week for from six months to a year agreed to come to Sydney University for study. Significant hearing losses were measured in many of them.

Musicians, naturally, are even worse off than listeners. Of 15 rock musicians tested by Tennessee's Dr. Lipscomb, 10 had notable hearing losses for high-frequency tones. A saxophone player, aged 19, after five years in rock bands, had hearing no better than that of the average man in his sixties.

When guinea pigs were subjected to rock music at sound levels comparable to those heard in discotheques, some hair cells in the organs of Corti were partially collapsed, others totally collapsed, and still others displaced or missing.

The breaks provide the relief that save rock addicts and musicians from even greater hearing loss. When bands repeatedly take time off, the paying customers are irritated, instead of being grateful. The longer and more frequent the breaks, the better off the listener and performer.

While it may seem absurd to suggest that the teenager listening to rock does so from a desire for quiet, psychiatrists are saying just that. He may be much troubled by noise. The music, which he has selected, protects him from hearing noise produced by outside forces that he cannot control. In addition, he is asserting himself. No one else's will is being imposed upon him.

He is not only shutting out the unpleasant sounds of the outside world, he is also removing himself from the demands of other people. In this sense, rock has a function not too different from that of drugs.

Playing the high-fidelity system at very high volume, as some adults do, may serve a similar protective role. Even if the music is Beethoven and thus socially approved, the sound may reach levels that could be damaging over the long run.

Many people, carry small transistor radios with them wherever they go. Like the rock or classical record, the transistor substitutes selected sound for the unwanted. Achieving this personal peace at the expense of others is now being banned in one city after another. Those who would listen in public places must use earphones.

Epictetus' aphorism about listening rather than speaking can be applied with difficulty in many surroundings today. Long before noise damages hearing, it hampers communication. Once the background sound passes 50 dBA, a speaker must raise his voice by three decibels for each 10 decibels of noise. This is for tête-à-tête conversation. Should the level reach 90 decibels, a person two feet away from the speaker will not hear anything less than a shout. At 100 decibels, the shout must be directed into the ear of the listener. People instinctively raise their voices against background noise and the step-by-step increase has become the recognized physical phenomenon, the "Lombard effect."

"The cocktail party provides a critical test of listening to a talker against extraneous sound sources. . . . We brought the problem to the laboratory," wrote Irwin Pollack and J. M. Pickett in the staid *Journal of the Acoustical Society of America.* They questioned whether the noise might be "a health hazard for diplomats, bartenders, and other habitual party goers."

Party decibel levels of 80 to 85 "are not quite high enough to cause permanent impairment of hearing," revealed further research carried out by William R. MacLean at the Polytechnic Institute of Brooklyn.

He explained: "If guest A talking to listener X tries to outshout another guest B, A is ill-mannered. A is not ill-mannered if only trying to outshout general background noise."

Whatever the humor in making acoustical measurement of cocktail parties, these studies do focus attention on a key aspect of noise pollution: It changes human relationships. One person cannot talk meaningfully to another against loud background noise. An even greater quiet is needed for the individual to take stock of himself and formulate his philosophy.

Stand in a completely soundproofed room, shielded from traffic, airplanes, voices—and the sound of one's own heartbeats becomes audible, an exciting beat. The blood circulating through the body pounds in the ears. The movements of the intestinal tract can be heard. John Cage, composer of electronic music, has said that the silent moments during the performance of a musical work are not silence, that there is music in the working of the nervous system. Only in the presence of such silence on the outside is it possible to listen to the lost music of one's inner world. For most people today, noise has drowned out these sounds and much of the quieter music of the world outside as well.

CAN MAN ADAPT 6
TO NOISE?

A THREE-YEAR-OLD CHILD *with a heart defect lived in a house 500 feet away from a ten-horn fire siren. Sometimes when the alarm sounded, the little boy went into spasms. Any one of these, doctors warned, might prove too much for his faulty heart to endure. Fire department officials in the small New Jersey community decided to move the siren to protect him from the noise.*

That child was ill, and the danger to him was clear. But what could the siren—in either its former or present location—do to the well people in the community? Noise is being associated with a variety of physiological ills, in addition to hearing loss, affecting individuals who are basically healthy. Not ears alone, but the entire system is aroused and altered by noise.

"Noise is never casually ignored. It is analyzed at the highest level of the brain. If ignored, it is done so by choice," Dr. Welsh of the Friends Medical Scientific Research Institute, has said, and this may be at the root of the problem.

Noise tells each person where he is in his world. It can add information to that being brought in by the eyes and other senses, or be the forerunner, presenting the first clues about a new event. The body is equipped with a set of auditory muscular reflexes. As sound enters, they cause the head and eyes to turn toward the source. The listener prepares to respond as he should. The baby cries in the next room and his parents come running. A friend's voice is heard calling from across the street before he is seen. The traffic noise gives the distance and location of the highway.

At the most basic level, noise comes as a warning—of danger, disaster. In the jungle the roar reveals the lion's presence; in a modern city the blast of a horn and the screech of brakes give evidence of a car bearing down; in the street, a scream tells that someone is frightened or hurt.

At the sound the entire body rises to meet the challenge. The initial reaction of the person menaced by noise is much the same as that of one menaced by a threatened blow. The eyes blink, pupils dilate, skin pales, and the face grimaces. The breath is drawn in and held. Knees bend and the head alone, or head and body, jerk inward and forward. Both voluntary and involuntary muscles tense. Normal inhibitions are overridden by the sudden massive demands placed on the nerve fibers leading to the brain.

The heart rate of the starling speeds when recordings of distress calls are played to him, as does that of the frog listening to meaningful ultrasonic signals inaudible to many other creatures. The circulatory system of man also displays striking responses to noise; heart rate fluctuates and blood pressure rises. When sound levels pass 70 decibels, blood vessels in the extremities constrict, making fingers and toes feel cold, while at the same time blood flow to the brain increases. The adrenal and pituitary glands, which govern a host of body functions, are stimulated and adrenal epinephrine, ACTH, and other hormones come rushing into the bloodstream. At the same time the liver releases glucose for quick energy. The skin's resistance to electrical impulses is altered. The body fluids undergo changes in chemical makeup and in quantity. The dry mouth of stress or fear is evidence of a fall in the amount of gastric juices and saliva being secreted. The stomach churns, as abdominal muscles contract and the movement of the gastrointestinal tract abandons its normal patterns.

The main psychological reaction to noise is fear, a fear that magnifies all physiological reactions.

Long after a noise has stopped, the sound-induced changes are still fading. The quiet that follows is stimulation of a sort, too, requiring renewed adjustment.

If man were able truly to adapt to noise, then all these reactions would make little difference in the long run. But complete adaptation would be undesirable. Should an individual cease to respond to noise, he would not avoid the car speeding toward him, run out of the building at the fire alarm, come to the help of a screaming child. Instead, he is startled each time he hears the warning.

Rats were alarmed repeatedly with bursts of 119-decibel sound at one-minute intervals for 27 hours. The rats still responded with a startle reflex. The magnitude of the reflex lessened, but even when the animals were seemingly too exhausted to respond, they did so anyway.

Humans adjust somewhat better. A National Academy of Sciences-National Research Council study committee found that "responses to noise (excluding changes in hearing) . . . can adapt out with continued exposure." As a sound continues, it no longer sounds so loud. A contributing factor to such adaptation is fatigue, which in this context means that the listener's sensitivity to a sound has been reduced. The turn of head and eyes to orient a person to the noise gradually wanes. After 20 repetitions, it ceases. But this is habituation, the getting accustomed to a noise, not true adaptation.

Can man adapt to noise? **55**

If a sound is not heard for a while and then is repeated, the reaction returns in full force. Were there adaptation, the response would be less with each recurrence.

The reaction to noise is in part psychosomatic. Abraham Lincoln's famous dictum that some of the people can be fooled some of the time can be applied to the individual reactions to noise: You can get all people used to some noises and some people used to all noises, but you cannot get all people used to all noises.

A city dweller moved to a house across from a railroad station. "It took a long time for the trains to go away," he said, "but in time they did." But not necessarily for his neighbor. For some people, the trains will never go away.

No one will adjust to noise, whether of plane, truck, jackhammer, or rock music if it continually breaks into conversation and disrupts activities. The more often it happens, the more annoyed he becomes. Certain types of noise remain associated with fear. The individual becomes less rather than better able to endure the repetition; he is spent by the stress. Even if the fear is invalid, the tension it produces is as great. The barking dog may not bite, but the timid listener quakes, nonetheless.

Granted that many things happen to the body of the person who hears a loud noise, is it bad for him? Are the levels of noise to which millions are exposed every day damaging health as well as hearing?

Coronary heart disease, a common ailment in the civilized world, is unknown to the Mabaan tribesmen of the Sudan, the same natives whose hearing was found to be exceptional by Dr. Samuel Rosen. Hypertension does not occur: Blood pressure is the same for a 75-year-old Mabaan as for his 15-year-old grandson. Dr. Rosen saw no signs of atherosclerosis, varicose veins, duodenal ulcer, or ulcerative colitis. Some Mabaans have abandoned the quiet pastoral life to seek their fortunes in Khartoum where they for the first time endured noise and the other stresses of city life. With the passage of years they lost their apparent pastoral protection, and heart disease and hypertension were seen.

Animal studies provide additional indications that industrialization and noise are heart-disease linked. Rabbits were exposed to 120-decibel levels for 10 weeks. Although their diet was the same as that of other rabbits in quieter surroundings, the cholesterol in their blood reached higher proportions. High serum cholesterol has been implicated as a cause of heart disease in humans. Many of these rabbits became ill with atherosclerosis. Animals in a University of Western Australia laboratory developed hypertension after being forced to hear noise. Blood pressure continued to be higher than normal for some months after their return to quiet.

"There is some evidence that workers exposed to high levels of noise have a higher incidence of cardiovascular disease, ear-nose-and-throat disorders, and equilibrium disorders than do workers exposed to lower levels of noise," declared the Environmental Protection Agency report of December 31, 1971, to the President. This report was based on the results of a year's study and public hearings in eight cities.

Heart problems were diagnosed in about one in four of a thousand German workers in very noisy factories. This compares to roughly 15 percent for individuals in less noisy plants. Circulatory disorders were present in 60 percent of the first group, and half of the second.

N. N. Shatolov reported in *Russian Laboratory Hygiene and Occupational Diseases* that high blood pressure and heart abnormalities were frequent among 300 workers regularly exposed to industrial noise of 85 to 120 decibels. The electrocardiogram readings of heart action showed most changes at the end of the work day, and looked much like those produced by physical stress. The heart and blood pressure problems occurred most often and were more extreme in men who spent considerable time in the noisiest parts of the factory

Can man adapt to noise? **57**

where the levels ranged from 114 to 120 decibels.

When a thousand workers in another Soviet factory were questioned, a surprisingly large number complained of feeling poorly. Physical examinations turned up many cases of hypertension and of peptic ulcer.

"The Soviets seem more concerned with the nonauditory physiological effects than with the auditory effects," noted a representative of the Environmental Protection Agency after a visit to the U.S.S.R.

The legal limit for industrial noise was lowered by five decibels recently, chiefly for physiological reasons, other than hearing. Soviet noise researchers spend most of their time nowadays investigating cardiovascular and central nervous system changes.

Some years ago a strange reaction, seemingly unrelated to noise, occurred in a man who had worked for many years in a metal foundry where sound levels often were higher than 110 decibels. His eyes, rather than ears, circulatory, digestive, or nervous systems, were affected. There were changes in the size of his field of vision. The worker sought help from eye doctors in vain. Since then, this disability has been observed a number of times. In some individuals with prolonged noise experience of 130 or more decibels, nystagmus, a rapid, involuntary eyeball movement, can result.

Even sound that is not heard can cause discomfort. Nausea, fatigue, and vertigo may be due to the resonance of very low-pitched sounds in the internal organs. Motors turning slowly can generate at infrasound frequencies. Many airlines mask with music the infrasound emitted by idling engines before takeoff. The person affected by low-frequency sound may not know what is bothering him.

A more recondite effect of noise—an inability to fight off illness —appeared in mice, harassed by loudspeaker blasts, at the University of California's Brain Research Institute. A dose of virus that would normally be lethal was injected into the noses of 249 mice.

Then for the next three hours noise of 120 to 123 decibels blared through a loudspeaker. Death struck down 188 of these mice, compared with 108 of a second group of the same number which had been sick in quiet surroundings. The stress of noise had brought about a significant decrease in the protective inflammatory response. In addition, the cells produced less interferon, a chemical that helps to combat viral invasion. Blood counts revealed a marked decline in the leukocyte cells that are also important in producing resistance to illness.

Animal studies and observations of humans point to a host of disabilities, aside from deafness, in people exposed to noise. Still, the consensus report by the Environmental Protection Agency cautions: "The effects of noise on people have not been successfully measured in terms of excess deaths, shortened lifespan, or days of incapacitating illness. There are only hints that such effects might exist."

"If it were possible to take a person who had never experienced noise and run a battery of physical and psychological tests and then, keeping him in the exact environment, add noise, and some years later do a second series of tests, these might tell us something," explained a noise expert, adding, "even then, the passing years themselves affect all body systems."

The higher incidence of illness and disabilities among people in noisy surroundings could be blamed, said the Environmental Protection Agency, on such non-noise matters as age, dust levels, occupational danger, or life habits.

The Russian and German industrial workers may have had hypertension and heart trouble before they were employed in the factories investigated. Perhaps men in the noisiest surroundings could not get other jobs. Ventilation and lighting may have been poor, and heavy physical tasks demanded that were beyond the strength of these individuals. The frequently cited Mabaan tribesmen have not been subjected to controlled study. Those who left the idyllic rural setting might have been the malcontents of the tribe, people who would be particularly susceptible to heart disease and hypertension.

Even the animal studies can be questioned. In some of the earliest and most basic studies, certain strains of rats, mice, and other rodents were exposed to sudden loud noise. After an initial startle response, they began running about, then made jerky steps or pivoted head and body. In just 15 to 20 seconds, they were having full-fledged convulsions. But, with the exception of some epileptics, sudden noises do not trigger seizures in people. This raises the question of whether other animal experiments on the effects of noise can be extrapolated to man.

Still, research in all fields of medicine is based on the animal model. And virtually every major discovery has involved preliminary use of nonhuman subjects.

It will take many years to investigate all the aspects of noise and its effects, first on animals and then man, and populations are exposed to noise in the meantime.

"Legal noise limits should be set intuitively without waiting for all results of research," declared Dr. Welsh. "Enough information exists when coupled with common sense."

On this basis limits are being imposed on factory owners and manufacturers of noisy products. Some animal lovers think the same common sense should be applied to beast as to man. Sound levels inside a typical open-rail pigpen are as high as those on train platform or assembly line. One noise-control engineer has urged that pigs and other animals be covered by the noise regulations designed to protect man.

THE ANIMAL MODEL 7

THE LAPLANDERS *do not keep large herds of reindeer in corrals at times when nature is noisy. During thunderstorms the animals are let out to roam at will. If crowded together, they are likely to stampede.*

Most information about the effects of noise on animals has not been gathered on ranches or farms, but rather in laboratories. As a rule, animals serve as models for humans. Sometimes the guinea pig, rat, or mouse stands in for fellow creatures of the wild and on farms whose reaction to sound intrusion is harder to measure.

Animals exposed to noise in the laboratory have displayed a host of disturbances ranging from hypertension to hormonal imbalance. Even death has been reported—although this is actually an indirect result. Mice have been killed by a 160-decibel siren. The heat produced by the sound energy is too much for furry animals to withstand.

The most obvious effect of noise on animals, as on humans, is harm to hearing and deafness has been produced in monkeys, dogs, cats, chinchillas, rats, and guinea pigs. A variety of loud noises, including those of helicopter rotor, tailpipe blast of jet aircraft, sonic booms, and gunshots, was played for squirrel monkeys and guinea pigs. Postmortem studies showed clear signs of damage in the sensory cells of the inner ear, as well as the adjacent nerve endings and hair cells. In some animals the membrane had been ruptured.

Of all animals, the monkey is the most like man. It is hard for humans to focus attention in the presence of noise. Similarly, when eight monkeys were forced in a test to listen to high-intensity jet engine noise, they became disoriented and nauseous.

The young champanzees at the London Zoo show signs of terror at sonic booms, though the reaction does not last long. "Alertness and momentary concern" characterize most other animals in the San Diego Zoological Garden, but "peacocks invariably sound off," the director wrote to a National Academy of Sciences subcommittee investigating animal responses to sonic booms. "Mammals, for the most part, are not vocal, but obviously show an awareness."

Animals signal one another of the coming of danger. Noise thus serves as a warning to them as it does to man. Sometimes their response is not apparent in human terms, yet physiological tests have shown how alarmed they really were.

"Many rats appeared almost unconcerned by loud noise. Yet they displayed enlargements of the adrenal glands and the thymus, declines in the thyroid, and gonadal impairment," Dr. A. Stanley Weltman of the Research Institute at the Brooklyn College of Pharmacy told an environmental agency hearing.

To see whether the general health of animals on the farm would be as affected by noise as is that of laboratory animals, some early weaned lambs were reared in Kansas in ambient sound levels of 75 decibels and others in noise of 100 decibels. More weight was gained by those living in the quieter quarters.

While noise can be harmful to animals, music, to paraphrase the truism, appears to have charms to soothe the savage beast. A music camp was located on a Tennessee cattle farm. During the summer when the campers' orchestra was playing, the Black Angus would amble up to the studio. "By the end of the rehearsal," the camp director told an interested newspaper reporter, "the cattle would be right up at the front door listening. They really seemed to like the music."

The effect of noise on pigs, whether swilling, rooting, or mating, has been subjected to intense study. "These trials invariably led to the conclusion that swine are almost entirely indifferent to loud sound during mating," reported Dr. James Bond after the Agricultural Research Service had observed and taken motion pictures of the animals copulating while sound of high intensity was introduced.

Mink were equally oblivious during sexual activity. "The mating ritual was not disturbed. Pairs seem oblivous to sonic booms once copulation began," wrote Wilson B. Bell of the Virginia Polytechnic Institute and State University.

It would appear logical for noise to be more disturbing during the less absorbing activities that follow mating. A variety of experiments has proven that it does . . . does not . . . or does temporarily.

When Jersey cows are frightened by exploding paper bags during milking, the flow stops. Within 30 minutes, however, it is possible to remove 70 percent of the normal amount from the udder by hand milking. Flyovers have not been shown to have any effect on milk production of 42 herds near Lockbourne Air Force Base, Ohio. Dairy cows reacted to only 19 of 104 booms, and in a relatively minor way.

A Japanese researcher, on the other hand, has described most dire results of noise. The din from motorboat racing caused a remarkable decline in milk yield on a nearby dairy farm, reported Ryosuke Oda, assistant professor of livestock science, Yamaguti University. Most of the cows became nervous and reacted even to very slight noises. Many stayed on their feet all day. The animals grew thin. Their reproductive capacities were affected, and artificial insemination with semen purchased at the Prefectural Live-Stock Hygiene Service Station was unsuccessful unless repeated four to six times. Dr. Oda then described the sad case histories of "Osma," sold because she became so irritable, and "Sakota," whose milk lessened in quantity, and eventually she died, still young. "Tiche's" milk yield also greatly decreased, while "Lyen" ceased to lactate, then "suffered from the nervousness and finally was mad." American agricultural specialists think noise alone could not have produced these calamities. It might, however, have contributed to the cows' decline.

Some experts maintain that animals on farms are not damaged by noise, while others support claims by farmers against noise producers.

"In the opinion of the court there is a causal relationship between the overflight and the abortion," held a Norwegian court deciding a charge of injury brought by a fox farmer. The veterinarian who had been called in could "not think of any other cause than the low flight with much noise. The farm has had excellent results both before and after the event."

In 1941 the Nord Gudvrandsdal circuit court heard fox farmers' testimony about a mother fox destroying her newborn whelps following blasting. "The person who does the blasting . . . must be prepared to be held responsible [for mishaps occurring]. . . . Thus it has, for example, been forbidden to fire salutes between 1 May and 17 May in districts where silver fox breeding is widespread."

"It is an old experience that psychic influences can cause abortion in fur animals in captivity," wrote Finn Gjesdal in a Norwegian veterinary journal. He pointed to evidence that foxes in particular are extremely sensitive to the effect of loud noise and that abortion and the biting to death of newborn have resulted. Animals on a fur farm might become so anxious that they neglect their whelps instead of suckling them.

The Norwegians regard mink as less sensitive than silver foxes. Nonetheless, the most carefully controlled noise tests have been made on mink farms. In 1970 a joint experiment was carried out by the Department of Agriculture, the Universities of Alaska, and Washington, and the Air Force on the southern end of Mitkof Island, Alaska. About 200 healthy female and 50 male mink were boomed by military aircraft from Elmendorf Air Base at Anchorage. The jets traveled at supersonic speed to produce a pressure wave of close to six pounds per square foot as it hit the ground.

"This is a boom that shakes the earth. The observers were pretty much shaken up," said Dr. Bond, who was present. "There were three booms within an hour and a half. By the third boom, the minks were not even looking up. I saw one nursing mother continue to suckle. The camera recording the action of the minks twisted as a result of the boom. The mother at first stuck her head out of the kennel. Then she went back to the kits.

"Noise does not seem to disturb animals as much as it does humans," he continued. "They are very adaptive to noise in a hurry. I know of no scientific proof that mink have ever eaten their young due to noise. This does not mean it might not have happened; but we have not seen it. We put our animals under the greatest possible stress, and none ate her young. And we had cameras covering them, so any such action would have shown up."

Mink in Scandinavia beneath the flight paths of subsonic planes also were comparatively unconcerned. No kits were lost. Two of the mothers brought their babies out of the box, but then returned them, and another blocked the entrance to her box with straw.

On the other hand, a mink breeder in England was awarded £7,500 after suing that the Concorde's sonic boom made his minks "nervous wrecks." They went into a panic; "some carried their young on their backs." He claimed to have lost 1,700 animals.

An American court allowed recovery for mink frightened by airplanes. Minnesota farmers charged that the mink had destroyed their young, and were made worthless as breeders. A construction company was found legally responsible for injury to mink terrified by a noisy steam shovel. A mink rancher was granted his request that the Minnesota Livestock Sanitary Board investigate whether heavy kit mortality in 1966 and 1968 was due to the sonic booms.

But the legal situation is far from clear-cut. Another rancher who claimed that his mink were frightened by blasting did not win his case.

During the fiscal years 1961–1970, 238 claims involving animals and sonic booms were made against the Air Force. Of these, 49 pertained to chickens, 43 to horses, 38 to mink, and 32 to cattle. Payments were made on 98 of the claims, including 20 for harm to cattle, 23 to chickens, 20 to mink, and 17 to horses.

Most of the animals had been hurt when trampling, jumping through fences, stampeding, and crowding following noise-induced panic. A pony broke his leg, and a dog ran through a glass door after a sonic boom. In each case damages were paid.

Courts take into consideration whether a horse frightened by noise remains too skittish to be ridden or driven later. According to one judgment cited by Harold W. Hannah, professor of agriculture and veterinary medical law at the University of Illinois, "Animals are not given to deceit or malingering and damage by fright can be proved without proving physical impact."

Poultry, particularly when unaccustomed to noise, has reacted to sonic booms by scattering. Broilers and young turkeys get particularly excited. During one sonic boom test the number of pheasant eggs declined. But cautious veterinarians would not say whether the boom or excessive heat and a heavy molt were to blame.

The Air Force responded to claims brought by hatchery men with tests at White Sands Proving Grounds. A total of 3,415 eggs was exposed to booms during different parts of the 21-day incubation period. The number that hatched was roughly the same as is normal and no developmental deviations were observed.

Animals clearly do not cooperate with investigators. The exact opposite of the Army finding, a drop in egg production following three days of stress, was reported in a poultry trade journal. The hens had probably become too disturbed to eat and drink the quantities they needed. When henhouse noise reached discotheque levels, 11 of 12 brood hens being observed stopped sitting on their eggs.

Noise may affect egg production by acting on prospective father rather than prospective mother. Pullets on an experimental farm were inseminated with sperm from male fowl, which had been exposed to aircraft noise of 120 decibels. The hens remained in quiet surroundings. Yet when the eggs from that breeding were hatched and counted, the number was smaller than usual.

OF WILDLIFE, PLANTS, AND THE BALANCE OF NATURE 8

THE LITTLE COTTON RAT, Sigmodon hispidus, *lives in the pine-palmetto-grasslands that surround the Cape Kennedy Regional Airport at Melbourne, Florida. The animal neither migrates from the area nor becomes torpid during the winter months, but endures the noise of jet planes landing and taking off down the nearby runways all year around.*

This species of rat suddenly gained prominence when it was selected by the local planning council as test animal to determine the possible ecological impact of the airport. During the time the animal's habits were being considered, 18 landings and as many takeoffs occurred each day.

Population density was determined by the number of rats that entered traps, baited with peanut butter and oat flakes. Larger traps with equally attractive lures for oppossums, skunks, bobcats, and foxes were set to discover how many remained in the area. An average of only 2.58 cotton rats per acre was calculated for the high-noise corridor, a wet area near the runway. Yet only a few hundred feet away in the dry palmetto-grassland, the number of rats was 10.3 per acre. The two areas are almost equally noisy, yet noise may, nonetheless, explain the difference in populations. Burrows can be dug in the dry ground, but not in the wet. Thousands of gopher turtle burrows were found in the dry areas near the airports. It is common for gopher mice and gopher frogs to borrow turtle burrows and they were seen climbing in and out. The cotton rat is not usually a burrow dweller, but may have taken over here in order to escape the loud noise.

The emotional state of the rats is also affected by the noise. Those rats that lived nearest the runways were found to be more timid than others. Only five of eight would leave an open jar to run across a field, while all 12 from a region three-fourths of a mile away from the runways were bold enough to venture out. The rats from the airstrip were also less sociable than their fellows from quieter regions. When placed in a box with another rat, 27 minutes on the average passed before any contact at all was made. The rats from the more distant point were making friends in about nine minutes. The runway animals were also hesitant to press noses with a companion or engage in mutual grooming activities.

Although the planning council warned that these tests are by no means complete, it does appear that "general behavior differences exist between the two groups."

The larger traps caught no bobcats or foxes, and extremely few big mammals of any other kind. Some spotted skunks were trapped and even these were taken most often at a site five miles from the airport. The presence of a noisy airport, surrounded by housing developments and traffic, probably led those larger mammals that could get away easily to do so. As they have left the area, it is probably only a matter of time until predatory reptiles and birds increase in number and take over.

This study, however fragmentary, is one of the few that has been made anywhere to date that considers the possible effect of noise on the ecosystem of an era. It might seem to be of little consequence whether cotton rats are numerous, bold, or loving, or whether snakes replace foxes. But nature is in a fine state of balance which depends on a host of seemingly unimportant interrelationships. Any change can bring trouble. One chilly New England spring the caterpillars were scarce; lacking their main source of food, birds died by the thousands. In places where the praying mantis has been wiped out, the harmful insects it would have consumed increase in number and damage plant life.

"It is quite likely that there are many effects of noise on wildlife, but there are hardly any such studies of animals in their natural habitat. Nor is there evidence to show how they lived before noise was added. Most situations are investigated after the fact. The literature in the field is neither abundant nor highly qualified," said Professor John L. Fletcher, of Memphis State University's Department of Psychology, who was called in to survey writings on the subject for the Environmental Protection Agency.

"There has been little or no consideration of the range of hearing. Most research is carried out in the human range of 20 to 20,000 Hz, but animals have a different one. Bats, for example, hear signals of from 125 to 150,000 Hz."

Other animals are attuned to very low or very high frequencies only.

"The natural reaction to a suddenly arising situation is flight," wrote the Norwegian, Gjesdal. A loud noise thus could drive animals away from nesting grounds or into unusual habitats.

For many years the 40,000 pairs of Dry Tortugas Sooty Terns nesting in Florida produced about 25,000 to 30,000 fledglings during the hatching season. Then in 1969 came a season of disaster when hardly a fledgling was hatched. The failure rate amounted to 99 percent. That year low-flying supersonic military aircraft passed over the nesting area repeatedly, and in the opinion of Dr. W. B. Robertson, Jr., a research biologist with the National Park Service, the resulting sonic booms were responsible for the hatching failure. The booms may have damaged the eggs, a possibility discounted by some physicists because of the shape. It is more likely that the mother birds became panic-stricken and flew away from their nests.

One January three or four ravens were flying over a remote upland valley in central Wales. Suddenly there was a sonic boom. The birds called in agitated tones and others flew in from all directions. Within five minutes at least 62 were counted by an observer, some must have traveled for two or three miles to reach the scene of the disturbance. Half an hour later 30 or more ravens were still uneasily circling the valley.

Yet one can often see birds nesting on airport runways, and in some places rabbits jump out of the way of planes at landing and takeoff. This cannot be taken as proof that noise is harmless to wildlife.

"Starlings and blackbirds and certain other kinds of birds do frequent airports, because they easily find food there, and they can tolerate the noise. But you do not see a great variety," explained Dr. Fletcher. "Others must move out. Few stimuli are aversive to all kinds of systems. Logically some organisms can survive under any given set of conditions. I do not think you will see robins, wrens, or bluebirds around airports."

Not only the air and the earth, but even the seas are not free of mechanical noise intrusion. The works of man can match the natural sounds made by many of the creatures of the seas. In late May, 1970, Drs. William C. Cummings and Paul O. Thompson of the Naval Undersea Research and Development Center, sighted four blue whales under the waters off Isla Fuafo near the coast of Chile. The sounds made by these animals were recorded and found to be exceptionally low in pitch, from 12.5 to 200 Hz.

Of wildlife, plants, and the balance of nature **71**

"These underwater moanings were the most powerful sound recorded for living animals—188 decibels at one meter," they reported.

Powerful for animals perhaps, but easily equaled by technology. The sound is "the same overall noise level as that of a United States Navy cruiser traveling at normal speed."

The argument over the supersonic transport plane has centered on the need to protect people from the sonic boom. Emphasis has, therefore, been placed on prohibiting such aircraft from flying over land. Yet the seas are not untenanted. The Citizens League Against the Sonic Boom has reported letters of protest signed by 39 oceanographers and marine biologists from Woods Hole Oceanographic Institute and Marine Biological Laboratory. "No adequate answers are available to questions as to the possible harm of such booms, known to be startling to men and animals, to life above and below the surface of the ocean."

The sonic boom is only the latest threatened human intrusion into the animal world. On rare occasions, some creature makes trouble. During World War II, the snapping shrimp, *Alpheidae,* unexpectedly became an object of interest to naval experts. The crustacean makes a loud crack by closing a highly specialized large claw. This sound interfered with sonar.

Engineers can cope with such problems; when animal communication is disrupted mechanically, results may be devastating. Animals recognize mates, predators, and prey by means of noise signals, some vocal, others made by various parts of the body. The gorilla beats its breast, the wood pigeon its wings, and the stork snaps and clatters its bill. Birds may send complex messages, with one directing his call to a designated individual. By imitating the sound frequency range of an enemy, they catch him off guard and kill him. The Laniarus bird varies the intervals between calls and replies and alters the speed and intensity of signals in order to sound the alarm or tell where food can be found. A porpoise with eyes covered by rubber cups has swum without error through a maze, avoiding the sides by sending out sound waves.

Sound has as much, sometimes more, sexual meaning as appearance or smell, carefully designed scientific experiments have shown. The male mosquito has gone so far as to struggle to copulate with a tuning fork emitting the female's attracting tone. A female insect, *Ephippiger,* rushed to a loudspeaker issuing the sex signal of the male. She chose the loudspeaker over the actual male when he was standing by in silence. Some equipment operates at ultrasonic frequencies beyond the range of the human ear. They are not too high to confuse the cicada and other insects.

The most basic animal relationships depend upon sound. In a test of poultry mother love, a turkey was surgically deafened before laying eggs. When they hatched she was unable to differentiate the chirping of her chicks from that of predator birds. As a result, she killed her own. A mother hen abandoned her chick when it was placed under a glass bell where she could see it, but not hear its cheep. The noise made by man and his machines may drown out the sound of child or mate and have results unforeseen by those who produced the machinery responsible.

Some animals might starve. The bat, relying totally on echo location, is unable to find food when interference is produced by natural or mechanical means. Insects dislike noise and fly or crawl away, forcing birds to go hungry or move.

Man now freely enters areas that once were remote and inaccessible. The trail bike, dune buggy, motorcycle, and snowmobile crash through wilderness, beach, desert, and forest. What does this mean to animals in hibernation?

"I am sure that there could be no possible positive effects of snowmobiles going where animals hibernate," commented Professor Fletcher. "As to harm, we have nothing that could be accepted as proof. But if hibernation were broken, the animals would require more heat and food, and that would raise major problems.

"If anything should restrict the range and change the food availability, that could be dangerous, particularly for species approaching extinction. Steps should be taken. I am not an alarmist, but I am concerned that noise is not even considered when there is no margin for error within a species."

And he cited as examples: "The grizzly bear seems to be on the way out; the California condor and whooping crane are in trouble."

A number of botanists and environmentalists are taking the extreme position that the balance for plant, as well as animal, life might be thrown off by noise. The view is an extension of one held by many plant lovers that "growing things do better when you speak to them every day in a pleasant way."

Scientific efforts to prove this hypothesis have centered around exposing plants to a variety of sounds and observing each stage of maturation.

Wheat was "treated" with several different sound frequencies issued from loudspeakers during the growth season by Mary Measures and Pearl Weinberger of the University of Ottawa.

"The height, number of roots, number of tillers, and fresh and dry weights of the root and shoot systems were significantly larger in plants pretreated with sound," was their finding.

They speculated on the basic mechanism by which sound produces its effects. The frequencies used in the test gave forth energy on what would seem to be too low a level to do anything to the plant —it amounted to a billionth of the energy needed to break a chemical bond. But if the natural vibration in a specialized part of the grain cell were the same as that of the sound wave, then the effects of the tiny sound vibrations would be cumulative. In time larger vibrations could occur in the cell and these might cause changes in some biochemical or biophysical processes. The Canadian researchers also suggested that sound pressure may act upon the water within the cells. The plants were treated at a variety of temperatures, and the effect on germination was found to be greatest when the weather was cold enough to cause water expansion.

Foreign botanical journals describe other tests of the effects of sound on growing things. Ultrasonic frequencies unheard by the human ear stimulated the germination and growth of barley, sunflower, pine, spruce, and Siberian pea tree seedlings. The improvement in growth was accompanied and probably caused by increased activity of certain enzymes in the seeds and seedlings. The sound waves may have stimulated the enzymes.

Botanists bearing musical instruments and tape recorders have ventured into gardens and fields. A violin was played every day amid the mimosa plants and they grew more luxuriantly than before. And in the *Journal of Annamalai University,* Madras, India, was an account of music played for half an hour daily in the rice paddies. The plants surpassed their normal heights.

A more detailed analysis of sound patterns and plant growth was worked out by Dorothy Retallack of Denver, who presented recordings of classical, semi-classical, avant-garde, and rock music to ordinary garden and house plants placed in a closed cabinet with a loudspeaker at one side. The plants were exposed to hymns and to "La Paloma," to strings, and to steel drums, to jazz and to country western. Rock was played by such groups as Led Zeppelin and Vanilla Fudge. East Indian sitar music was performed by Ravi Shankar; Bach chorales were transposed to the organ.

The East Indian temple ragas aroused the most favorable response from all the plants used by Ms. Retallack—petunias, carnations, geraniums, beans, and squash. Blossoming richly, they leaned toward the speaker as if to seize it, reaching a 60-degree angle. Devotional music was played to bean plants. In three weeks they were about two inches taller than others grown in a quiet chamber. Leaves were luxuriant and roots sturdy. Jazz had a good effect on growth, too, while country western music was the only type to produce no reaction at all. Plants with three hours a day of dissonant atonal avant-garde music directed at them were shorter than those of the same species growing in silence. The most dramatic effects were observed among all types of plants exposed to acid rock. They leaned away from the sound, as if trying to escape, and would not bloom. By the end of three weeks they were dying. The morning glory drooped instead of climbing: the corn stalks bent in the middle, and the beans were stunted. Leaves of most plants were browning.

Could such responses alter the balance of nature? No one has tested plants with traffic or jet noise to determine whether its effects are comparable to those of acid rock in the Denver experiments. What of the rose exposed day after day to the sound of air compressors and sirens? What of animal forage, or farm crops growing beneath aircraft flight paths? Who can say? Pollution of other kinds has been shown to damage plants. Choked in automotive exhaust, they grow poorly at the side of the highway. Air pollution made a desert of the land around a copper smelter, and no one had foreseen this catastrophe.

A LAW AGAINST IT 9

"WE WERE INFORMED *that if there were any local restrictions concerning community noise, they would just move to another county or another region or another state to construct their plant, or where such nonsense as this did not exist," the president of a Dallas acoustical consultant firm told an Environmental Protection Agency hearing.*

He had been called in by a manufacturer to assist in planning an industrial plant surrounded by small houses for employees. The management view was that if the employees "wanted a job they would tolerate the noise produced by the twenty-four-hour operation of the plant."

The firm had also been asked to aid in planning a new airport to cover 18,000 acres and cost half a billion dollars. When the experts recommended that noise control be inserted in the overall building and fire code that was to regulate this and all future building in the area, "we were bluntly informed that noise and airports are synonymous and that people expected noise in that environment."

Noise-measurement instruments were purchased by the Dallas city government. The acoustical consultants offered their services without charge to train city employees in the use of the devices. "Our offer was declined with thanks."

Brought in to work out noise-abatement techniques within a factory, the firm was told to do just enough to keep management from violating the law.

It is commonly believed that regulation of noise in industry came early. Not at all. Even the obvious fact that workers in noisy factories became deafened was not considered important for decades after the industrial revolution. Practically everyone in a plant with steam boilers became hard of hearing. As a result deafness was known as "boilermakers' disease." Still, industry-induced hearing loss was ignored or considered a necessary concomitant of employment.

"I always had to shout to make my father hear; he worked in a sawmill."

In how many families has a similar sentiment been expressed? In how many is it still true today? A 1960 study of 103 Italian shipyard workers found the hearing of every riveter and caulker to be affected. An investigation of 5,127 skilled and unskilled workers in Australia showed one-third to have hearing losses greater than 45 decibels. Of several hundred American diesel-engine-room personnel, 15 percent had permanent threshold shifts of more than 20 decibels at any frequency, a 1965 report revealed. And by the time of these studies, conditions had improved over the past.

In 1948 a workman for the first time succeeded in collecting damages for partial deafness. Matthew Slawinski sued the J. H. Williams Company for the gradual loss of hearing suffered in his 20 years of employment. Even though he was able to continue in his job as a drop forge worker, the court held the company liable. Mr. Slawinski received the niggardly sum of $1,661.25, but the precedent had been set.

It quickly became apparent to management, however, that the courts were not going to require them to deal generously with noise-injured employees. For a number of years courts in many states held that a worker had to leave a noisy factory for some months to prove that his loss was permanent, a ruling that had the practical effect of preventing many workmen from complaining.

But gradually the public objection to such injustice forced a change in attitude.

"At one time the law said a person would not be compensated unless the physical damage resulted in making him incapacitated for earning a living. Now courts are taking the position: if your ability to enjoy life has changed, you are entitled to compensation," stated Dr. Harris, who is professor of electrical engineering and architecture at Columbia University. "Even if you can still operate the lathe, but cannot listen to music, you deserve damages."

Federal regulation of noise in industry came in 1969. Noise was then included under the regulations of the Walsh-Healey Public Contracts Act, applying to firms with government contracts amounting to $10,000 or more. An estimated 27 million workers were involved. The original act, passed in the 1930s, had until then concerned itself primarily with minimum wage, although some safety provisions were included and an amendment referred to excessive noise without setting limits. In 1971 the Occupational Safety and Health Act covered all firms engaged in or affecting interstate commerce. These employ another 55 million men and women. The Bureau of Mines that year adopted the same limits.

In all this legislation maximum sound levels were set at 90 dBA for an eight-hour day, 92 dBA for six hours of exposure, 95 for four hours, 97 for three, 100 for two, 102 for one and a half, 105 for one hour, and 115 dBA for quarter of an hour or less. Impulsive or impact noise must not be greater than 140 dBA. Should sound levels exceed these standards, a program protecting the hearing—most often by

A law against it   79

issuing ear protectors—is to be put into effect as an interim measure while basic ways of reducing sound levels are sought. If any state is not satisfied with the federal limit, it can, by agreement with the Department of Labor, do better on its own.

Opposition to the legal limit was soon expressed. Going into the country's industries with sound and hearing measurement equipment, a team from the National Institute for Occupational Safety and Health found that it takes just two to three years of daily exposure to 90 decibels of noise for hearing losses to begin to appear. These are mostly in the higher-frequency range and keep on increasing over a 15-to-20 year job experience. By then the maximum of the noise-induced high-frequency loss has been sustained, but the worker begins to develop hearing disabilities in the lower frequency end of the range. With data of this kind coming in, the Institute in 1972 assembled a group of acoustical specialists who recommended an 85 dBA noise limit for an eight-hour day. This is a concession to practicability; many industries could not reduce noise by another 10 decibels in order to achieve the ideal 75 dBA. Despite heavy Environmental Protection Agency backing of the very moderate recommendation, there was no rush to change this legislation.

Industry has responded to the laws, in some cases to the letter.

"The guidelines were Walsh-Healey for the plant employees with no concern for the comfort of the families who would be living nearby," said the Dallas acoustical consultant.

The issuing of formal guides for industrial sound levels had the odd effect of providing an excuse for noise in a nonindustrial setting. The attitude appeared that if it is good enough for the government, it is good enough for highway, school, airport, or community. Yet, the industrial noise levels are far too high for comfortable living. Community efforts to deal with the problem have a long history, but the laws have seldom been effective.

Today's anti-noise regulations derive from old common law. The earliest ordinances which could be applied to noise were those for committing a nuisance. While most cases brought to court in the past dealt with air pollution and bad smells, the applicability to noise is clear.

Typical was the 1628 case of *Jones* v. *Powell* in England where the court ruled: "A tannery is necessary for all wear shoes, and yet it will be pulled down if it is erected as a nuisance to others."

A British chief justice also ruled that "the rights of habitation are superior to the rights of trade, and whenever they conflict, the rights of trade must yield to the primary or natural rights."

These views, however, have seldom been given much weight. Even today, the British Minister of the Environment must obtain Cabinet approval for any legislation that might affect industrial development.

While efforts to control noise have until now stopped short of pulling down the tannery, practically every city and state government has passed legislation against committing a nuisance. The meaning of nuisance is even more difficult to determine than that of noise. And so while many nuisance suits have come to court, they have seldom brought satisfaction to anyone, reveals a study performed by Stuart F. Lewin for the National Institute of Municipal Law Officers.

Consistency is lacking. A court in New York, for example, invalidated an ordinance prohibiting any noise that was annoying. On the other hand, a California court agreed that a dance hall was a nuisance if "the crowd in it upset the neighborhood by the noise they make or the offensive language they use." In some areas church socials, free indoor public entertainment, and the playing of musical instruments anywhere between 11 P.M. and 7:30 A.M. have been held to be a nuisance.

When is the music from the merry-go-round delightful and when is it a nuisance? A Texas civil court based its decision on location, rather than decibels. Amusement park rides may not be set up in quiet residential areas.

In Illinois it is against the law to engage in "the beating of drums, playing of tambourines, or making music or noise . . . on streets or sidewalks." And in Pennsylvania, it is an offense to be "drunk, noisy, and disorderly."

Sound trucks are prohibited in many cities. Civil libertarians, Mr. Lewin pointed out, question whether this infringes the right of free speech. The regulation has thus been struck down as unconstitutional in some courts, but upheld in others.

Students tell of the college president who during the unrest of the 1960s ended a demonstration by the simple expedient of unplugging the sound equipment.

In one code after another, there have been prohibitions of "loud, excessive, unreasonable, and unnecessary noise"—although no one is sure what any of these terms means. Even the model local law drafted by the National Institute of Municipal Law Officers, and adopted by Houston, Buffalo, and some other cities, continues the ban on "loud and unnecessary noise."

There is some risk that this ordinance might be used to stop an individual from public expression of unpopular views. The more practical problem, though, is how to interpret so vague a law. Many communities in the United States have some sort of noise code. Most, to quote the Environmental Protection Agency, are "poorly written and are not enforced." In an entire year in the early 1970s not a single noise arrest, aside from automobile violations, was made in Los Angeles, which has a long list of regulations. And there are cities with fine noise ordinances on the books, but no employees trained to measure noise. Passing a community law is not necessarily the key to noise control.

When the rules work, as they do in Memphis, they have the backing of official and private citizen alike. Memphis was one of the first cities to enact a noise code. The story told is that some years ago a newspaper editor became ill and had to stay home from work. Every evening a girl who lived across the street had a date, and every evening she was not ready on time. Her boyfriend would sit in his car at the curb and honk the horn until she came out. The editor began to wonder how much more such unnecessary horn-blowing was going on in the city. When he recovered he prepared blistering editorials in the newspaper, and soon the public officials began to take notice. Policemen and firemen volunteered their spare time to the anti-horn drive. Posters were put up in stores as part of a publicity campaign. In 1938 all unnecessary horn-blowing was prohibited by law. Within two years the change was felt and Memphis became known as "the quietest city."

Yet according to the trade publication *Fleet Owner,* "Memphis' regulations are no more strongly worded than those of many other communities."

And Dr. Rosenthal, Columbia law professor and expert in noise legislation, agreed that it was not the law that quieted Memphis. "The same kind of legislation has been passed in hundreds of cities. It is the spirit, not the law. There was an 'esprit' in Memphis that led to enforcement of the law."

To force this "esprit" on those to whom it does not come naturally requires action on the federal level. National legislation to curb noise pollution has lagged behind that for air and water. It comes as a surprise to most well-informed people that the Office of Noise Abatement and Control in the Environmental Protection Agency was not established until 1970. Up to that time, noise requirements had been set for industry and certain government-sponsored housing projects only, and research and development of quieter transportation had been ordered. Air, water, and some other aspects of the ecology were to be considered in the environmental impact statements required of federal agencies under the National Environmental Policy Act of 1969. But noise was mentioned among these aspects for the first time the following year along with the order that the Environmental Protection Agency administrator review and comment in writing on all statements. Neither the administrator, nor the other officials required to read the statements and consider environmental impact, was given the power to cancel a project, however.

The Clean Air Act Amendments of 1970 did more than add the Environmental Protection Agency to the impact statement procedure. Under the same act, the new noise abatement and control office directed by Alvin V. Meyer, Jr., was required to hold public hearings and then issue a report to be used as the basis for a federal anti-noise law.

The Noise Control Act of 1972 was passed on October 18 of that year, as Congress prepared to adjourn, and was signed by the President on October 27.

With the passage of this law the federal government at last broadened its attack on the noise problem. "The Congress declares that it is the policy of the United States to promote an environment for all Americans free from noise."

The new law did not start out by setting noise standards. That came later. First some 18 months were devoted to studies and more public hearings on such noise sources as construction and transportation equipment, including recreational vehicles, any motor or engine, and electrical or electronic machinery. Not until the summer of 1974 were the first standards proposed for those products identified as most troublesome. With the Environmental Protection Agency given the power to regulate noise from interstate carriers, trucks and railway trains were in the initial group, along with air compressors. Particularly noisy products were to be labeled as such. Aircraft noise was considered separately, and the Federal Aviation Administration retained a good deal of its power. That agency, though, must consult with the Environmental Protection Agency administrator and the

Secretary of Transportation before setting standards for measuring aircraft noise and the sonic boom. It was ordered to refuse certification to any aircraft so noisy as to menace health. Any citizen was given the right to bring a suit against a noise producer or against the administrator of the Environmental Protection Agency, the Federal Aviation Administration, or any other government agency for failing to carry out the law. The sums budgeted to the Environmental Protection Agency for noise-control activities amounted to $2,014,000 in fiscal 1973, $4,292,000 the following year, and $8,797,000 in 1975.

As an ultimate goal, the agency has calculated how much noise people can endure without physical harm or excessive annoyance. This is compared to how much they actually do endure on a 24-hour basis. "We add up all the noise levels in an area, and penalize night sounds. A noise that measures 55 decibels would be counted that by day, but would be weighted to 65 at night," explained an Environmental Protection Agency spokesman.

Over the course of 24 hours the noise level should average 70 decibels or lower to prevent hearing damage. Inside schools, hospitals, and homes—whether in city, country, or on farms—sound should be no greater than 45 decibels. This amount of noise does not interfere with conversation and activities. Out-of-doors in residential, school, or hospital districts, the noise level should be held to 55 decibels, while around businesses, it can reach 75 dBA.

"This is what we need, not necessarily what we can get."

At present typical community noise averages 70 decibels. When sound heard at work, while traveling, running power mower or motorcycle is added, an individual's cumulative noise exposure reaches a higher level.

Future improvements will depend not only on how quiet the noise sources *can* be made, but how quiet they *will* be made. The agency pointed out that new products noise standards are based on three criteria: protection of health and welfare, technological feasibility, and economic feasibility. Although the level set for new trucks, for example, would still allow them to make noise above the annoyance level, driver and people living near highways would get some protection from hearing loss.

In order to set a good example, the agency ordered the government to purchase "low-noise emission products" as substitutes for noisier ones, provided the price differential were not too great.

Opposed by a number of interest groups, the bill as passed is a compromise version, based on a House of Representatives amendment to the more stringent Senate bill co-sponsored by Senators Edmund S. Muskie of Maine and John V. Tunney of California. Lost to the practical necessity of getting a bill approved were a number of provisions giving the Environmental Protection Agency more power over aircraft noise. And where the original Senate bill had provided for grants to state and local governments to support their noise-control programs, no funds were allotted. The budget was cut from the original $21 million to be allocated over three years—modest enough in comparison to the large appropriations for other forms of pollution control.

Still, as it stands the Noise Control Act represents a major change. It reflects the new attitude of Americans toward noise, an attitude that has survived the slackening of interest in the environment that accompanied the oil shortage and energy crisis. As Senator Tunney commented on the aircraft section: "It is not the intention of the Congress that the phrase 'economic reasonableness' continue to be interpreted as it has been in the past. . . . Congress intends that the reasonableness of the cost of any regulation or standard be judged in relation to the purposes of this act, which is to protect public health and welfare from aircraft noise." Perhaps the moment has come when the "rights of trade" will yield to the "rights of habitation."

Senator Tunney's office held an "oversight" hearing the spring following the act's passage and found "no ebb in public interest in noise . . . the public is getting steadily angrier."

Although states and cities are not receiving the funds that would make noise control easier, local governments are, nonetheless, affected by the setting of national standards and goals. It is not mere coincidence that within two years of the federal bill, some of the most stringent and far-reaching state and city codes have been passed. In these newer regulations limits for many types of noise are set in decibel counts, giving an answer at last to the question of what is "excessive."

In the past, New Jersey producers of excessive noise suffered fines of no more than $25, because noise was considered a local violation under disturbing-the-peace ordinances. In January, 1972, the nation's first statewide comprehensive noise-control law was passed. Since then violators have been at risk of $3,000 fines. Decibel limits were given for industrial noise; mufflers for cars and machinery were made mandatory; curfews were set on use of noisy equipment. Hours of quiet were listed, not to be broken by power mowers or garbage collectors.

Not only was a state environmental protection agency set up in Illinois, but also a pollution control board to issue orders and an Institute of Environmental Quality to provide technical assistance.

Chicago is notable among the cities for its precedent-breaking code passed in 1971. The theme of the city-sponsored advertising campaign was "SSSHHICAGO." Noise limits for cars and machinery are given in decibels, and new models are to be quieter than the old. Lawbreakers may be fined up to $500 and sentenced to six months in jail. Compliance is checked by traveling teams made up of two noise inspectors and a policeman. In the year June 1971–1972, 1,649 cases were brought to court. So vigorous are the members of the enforcing "Silent Service" that they refuse to grant exemptions even to churches. Too noisy chimes have been silenced. According to *Time* magazine, a rooster was ordered out of the northwest part of the city and into the country.

Bitterly fought by the building, transportation, and utility interests, a strict New York City anti-noise bill was passed in September, 1972. Opposition was most intense to the ban on construction noise before 7 A.M. and after 6 P.M., and on weekends. Decibel limits are set for air compressors, paving breakers, cars, and other machines. In a city where horn-blowing is considered a right by many drivers, claxons are to be adjusted mechanically so that they can make noise of no more than 75 dBA at a distance of 25 feet. In addition, horn-blowing is to be limited to signaling of "imminent danger." Even sirens are regulated—to a still noisy warning level of 90 dBA at a distance of 50 feet. Garbage compacting vehicles are to break the morning's peace with sound no greater than 70 dBA as heard from 10 feet away. New Yorkers have learned to dread the burglar alarm set off by cause or accident in building or car, screaming on for hours. The law requires an automatic turnoff after 15 minutes—time to capture the burglar or let him escape. The subway is to lose its unlimited noise license, with a year allotted to determination of what sound levels should and can be. Shopkeepers may not play music in the street to lure customers; radios or tape recorders may not be audible on public transport. Even the ice-cream vendor must keep his hands off the pull that makes the bell jingle and attract neighborhood children. Only one 10-second jingle per block is now allowed. The city's environmental protection administrator was allowed two years to divide New York into noise-quality zones and set sound levels for them.

Penalties for individual lawbreakers range from $50 to $500 for each violation for each day it continues, while businesses are assessed at a $500 to $2,000 daily rate. Noise-makers may also be given 30 days in jail. Citizens are encouraged to complain about noise producers. An imaginative provision has been written into the law allowing a citizen half of any civil penalty collected if he brings the action himself. Should the Environmental Protection Administration act on the citizen's complaint, he still receives a quarter of the fine.

To suggest that passage of the New York City code brought immediate silence to the city is an absurdity. Car burglar alarms are still so strident and continue for so long that an extremely deaf person recently complained about one. The "imminent danger" limitation on horn-blowing would be taken as a joke were it even recognized by many drivers. A trailer truck turning up 34th Street slowed traffic for a minute or so. Not the smallest danger was involved, yet it took but a second for every driver in the long line of cars to press his horn and keep on pressing it. In late spring of 1974, the subways were still so noisy that a suit was brought to the New York State Supreme Court requesting that the Metropolitan Transportation Authority be forced to reduce the "illegal and health-threatening levels" throughout the system. At Public School 98, close to the elevated tracks of the Seventh Avenue I.R.T., about one-tenth of each school day is lost for learning by students. But the suit was quickly dismissed on technical grounds.

The state of New Jersey could not be described as a haven of quiet either.

And New York and New Jersey possess some of the very best state and city codes. Taken as a whole, "the community ordinances are a curious lot," said Dr. Theodore J. Schultz, of Bolt, Berenek and Newman, engineering firm, Cambridge, Massachusetts. "A previous Chicago ordinance dating from the early 1950s is the base used by many cities. They have lifted out the regulations, even to the numbers. These do not apply in the same way to other areas. Anyone with a good lawyer can get out of them," he remarked at a meeting of the American Association for the Advancement of Science.

Sometimes the major source of noise is allowed free rein. In many

A law against it　**89**

communities daytime construction is exempted from control, in others, motor vehicles, Dr. Schultz pointed out. And occasionally an ordinance has been declared unconstitutional, because it would affect tourists unfavorably.

Some local governments have tried to cope with the noise problem by keeping businesses and homes apart through zoning regulations. In Chicago, for example, factories with noisy equipment may not operate within 200 feet of any residence. Chicago, St.Louis, and a number of other cities set a maximum noise limit at the line dividing homes from industry. On the other hand, a regulation in another Illinois city set sound limits at boundaries between commercial and residential districts and nothing happened as a result. An official explained the failure: "It was somewhat difficult to enforce. We had purchased a complex decibel meter, which was hard to operate."

Whatever the exceptions, most local governments are busy rewriting codes, and enforcing them. Whatever the weaknesses, in this current flurry of legislation lies the best hope for noise control. At the very least, the operator of the unmuffled air compressor at daybreak, the taxi driver leaning on his horn, the store owner blasting rock music onto the street is operating outside the law. The setting of decibel standards for many vehicles, machines, and equipment gives manufacturers a clear goal. Even if used too early or too late in the day, a comparatively quiet air compressor is less disturbing than a noisy one; even if thousands of cars go by, when each is quieter, the overall din is reduced.

If enough communities pass laws with means to enforce them, the harder it will be for plant owners to find sites where "such nonsense" does not exist.

Countries abroad are also recognizing the importance of noise control. Many have zoning codes listing specific distances between factories and homes. Noise control in England was included under the public health legislation in 1960. If three or more persons complain, a noise producer can be brought to court. The Greater London Council recently demanded a daytime maximum sound level of 75 dBA during construction work at County Hall. Every time the noise is louder than that for longer than 22 seconds, a bell goes off in the office of the "clerk of works," who can order a halt. The 22 seconds was considered long enough to allow for minor accidents, as a workman's dropping a hammer.

The U.S.S.R. has had noise-control legislation since 1956, and the Soviet model has been adopted by other Eastern European nations. A maximum of 85 dBA has been set for noise inside factories, while outside sound levels in populated areas are to be 55 dBA by day and 45 by night. A no-horn-blowing ordinance was passed in Moscow in 1956. Yet as has been found in many other places where anti-noise legislation is on the books, noise remains. The Soviet noise laws, according to a study made for the American Environmental Protection Agency, "in general are not strictly enforced." The government newspaper, *Izvestia,* in 1972 suggested that "life would be made easier for a lot of people by earplugs."

Still, in Tallinin in the Estonian S.S.R., there is a "commission on silence." Trucks may not be driven down residential streets after midnight, nor may they be loaded or unloaded between 11 P.M. and 6 A.M. A noise map of the city has been prepared by the Polytechnic Institute. With this as the guide, the municipal government has moved some factories away from the residential districts and has constructed a highway bypassing the city. Stores and workshops, now for the most part on the ground floors of apartment buildings, are to be relocated.

Tallinin has a "five-year plan" to create "wide and virtually deserted (to business) streets in the residential areas."

This kind of desert could never be created in the overpopulated cities of Asia where small industries are jammed up against housing.

In Japan factories making too much noise are given three years to get out of a residential district.

"This law is enforced when the people demand it. As soon as there is a complaint, we send an inspector," said a Japanese environmental official. "But sometimes if a small factory has been for many years in a place, mixed in with the residential area, the neighbors will accept the noise. They are friends."

JAPAN: THE WORST
NOISE, THE BEST LAWS

A NEW BUILDING *was going up in the Japanese city of Kyoto. Many people living nearby, particularly invalids and families with small children, moved to a hotel until the basic construction was completed. Hotel bills were paid by the owner of the new building.*

A succession of seemingly unrelated numbers flashes on the huge signs hung over the busy intersections of Tokyo. They might be taken for temperature readings, but the figures change too rapidly, going from one peak to the next. The numbers represent the decibels produced by the traffic.

Television is paid for by set owners, but when reception of the image is blurred by disturbance from aircraft, or voices are drowned out by noise, bills are reduced by about half.

Every city and community is divided into four zones, depending on use, with noise limits set for each in the daytime, morning and evening, and at night. The quietest levels are for zones near hospitals, schools, and old-age homes, while slightly higher decibel readings are allowed for the residential sections, and commercial areas can be noisier yet.

These are but a few examples of the heavy emphasis on noise control in Japan. Yet to walk down the streets of Tokyo, Osaka, Nagoya, or the other large cities of Japan is to experience sound as loud or louder than that heard in the United States. Bustling crowds push their way along sidewalks, talking in powerful voices. The streets are congested with many poorly muffled cars. Construction with antiquated equipment goes on for hours. Loudspeaker systems in trains and buses are pitched at extremely high levels. The screech of police car and ambulance sirens is more piercing than those in New York, though Japanese citizens say, "You should have heard them five years ago. They were even louder." Music, more often rock than Oriental folk songs, is played constantly and at full volume in public places.

For many aspects of noise control, the laws in Japan are the most advanced, specific, and imaginative of those passed in any country in the world. Yet the advanced law is one thing, the practice another. Japan serves as the perfect example of why noise control comes so slowly. Every noise problem faced by modern industrial nations is present, and in a most acute form. There is little land area, and so it is hard to find ways of moving people away from airports or factory zones. Houses lean upon one another and are made of wood with thin exterior walls and screen partitions within; many cottage industries or small factories are located in the very midst of housing. Urban planning, officials concede, is poor, compared to that in other countries. Large industrial complexes essential to the economy produce amounts of pollution too great for the small islands to absorb and there are busy international airports and car-choked highways.

Alongside all this, evidences can still be seen of the peace and repose that for centuries characterized the Far East. A dual strain runs through Japanese life and culture. The quality of life depicted in the painted scrolls and described in Haiku poetry and Noh plays and emphasized by the tea ceremony exists today, and the contemplative religions of the East have many followers. Cleanliness is prized to such an extent that a view of any city is in truth a view of laundry. Lack of hanging space inside homes puts the frequently washed clothing and linens over every roof and exterior wall. The smallest restaurant in Tokyo is spotless; the people are bathed. Train conductors appear in cream-colored uniforms, white muslin covers seats in taxicabs and chairs and sofas in business offices. Should a bit of land be free of house or industry, it becomes a carefully cultivated rock garden bringing a touch of beauty.

On the other hand, excessive crowding in the densely populated country makes it all but impossible for the city dweller to protect himself from noise. The Tokyo Metropolitan Research Institute for Environmental Protection recently found 709,000 people living in cramped houses, 56,000 with other families, 24,000 in nonresidential places, and 21,000 "in timeworn" dwellings. Most houses built before World War II were reasonably large, only about one-fifth had inadequate floorspace. Nearly half of those put up in the early 1960s occupy an area of 10 feet by 9.5 feet or less. Yet the average rent for a private house rose during the 1960s nearly five and a half times, an increase considerably greater than that for rice crackers, which nearly doubled in price, or pickled radish, which now costs two and a half times as much as it did ten years ago.

The scientists who prepared the report sought to arouse public opinion with dramatic tales of "tragedies caused by crowding." A mother lived with two infants in a three-mat (16-foot-square) house. One of the babies rolled over and in the tiny room became twisted in the television cord. The set fell and crushed him. A family of four had a single dark damp room in a wooden apartment building. Neighbors complained whenever the children cried. Leaving a farewell note, "I am sorry to have much troubled you, neighbors," the mother went out one day carrying her eldest daughter on her back and jumped in front of a train. Noise contributes to the tragedies of crowding; in a less drastic sense, it is one of the tragedies.

The Tokyo subways carry about 3,600,000 passengers a day; at rush hours "pushers" stand at each car door to provide what is needed to get the people in.

A national agency to deal with all aspects of pollution including noise was established by the "Basic Law for Environmental Pollution Control," approved in 1971. Air pollution has reached such catastrophic proportions in Japan that it receives the major share of attention and budget. Out of the agency staff of 500, only three are assigned to noise problems. Their instructions are that "levels of noise should be such that they will not disturb sleep, obstruct conversations, lower work efficiency and cause a disagreeable feeling." Not only sound, but also vibration is to be lessened.

"There is a very strict noise regulation, but it is one of the least observed of all laws. The government is too theoretical, too concerned with how to make laws. It does not act; it is a poor conductor of public opinion," stated an official of the environmental agency.

"Japanese people tend to be very egocentric," he continued. " 'If it does not affect me, it is all right,' so they do not do much about pollution themselves. They feel there is a law to control such noise."

"On the whole, I think complaints come from those who live in areas near highways or airports. People not troubled themselves are not much interested in whether other people are disturbed," added a staff member of the ministry of transport.

The flashing-light decibel counts over the intersections are dramatic. They give the public information. But no one in any government agency knew of any use being made of the information.

The environmental quality standards, similar to those issued by the Environmental Protection Agency in the United States, are invariably described by Japanese officials as "idealistic." They present a "goal," not a realistic or enforceable code. The listing in the legal document holds them as "standards . . . which are hoped to be maintained."

Nonetheless, when something the people care deeply about is involved, noise control is taken so seriously that it actually works. The visitor to Japan is repeatedly asked if he has yet ridden on the "bullet train." The pride and joy of government officials and citizens alike, it travels at 210 kilometers (130.4 miles) per hour, compared to 120 for the other trains, and it is always on time.

"Because of the speed it gives out great noise," explained Kazuo Arai, of the Railway Supervision Bureau, Ministry of Transport.

Ways of avoiding noise were considered from the moment construction of the first part of the line from Tokyo to Osaka began in 1964. Long rails were put down, rubber was placed between rail and railbed to absorb sound and vibration, and particularly effective springs were placed on the train itself.

"Still, people are grumbling about noise," said Mr. Arai.

There have been 120 complaints concerning railway noise since 1964. The number is misleading, because most were made by groups but counted as one, and only those formally accepted by the Ministry of Transport were counted at all.

The response to the complaints took a practical form: Walls were erected along the track of the original line in 15 places to protect schools, and in seven to shield hospitals.

"When the railway was extended from Osaka to Okayama, a distance of 165 kilometers [102.4 miles], a wall two meters [about 6.5 feet] high and 20 centimeters thick was built along the line. This was found to be the most suitable; three meters [about 10 feet] did not hold in the noise any better. The government pays for the wall and it is expensive. Ultimately one line will run through Japan from Sapporo in the north to Kagoshima in the south, and walls will surround the tracks."

Even aside from the highly favored railway, Japan is coming to grips with the noise problem in ways that other industrial countries might consider adopting. The prefectural (roughly equivalent to American states) and local governments are given the responsibility for noise control. Enforced regulation on the local level was, oddly enough, opposed at the outset by the Japanese government. Troubled because city regulations were stricter than the national laws of that time, "Some bureaucrats felt as if the metropolis rose in revolt against the government." But eventually the national "bureaucrats" gave way to those of "metropolis" and prefecture. The Tokyo pollution ordinance penalizes the most serious offenders with a year in prison or a fine.

Construction noise, if local rulings were followed to the letter, would be quite endurable: At a distance of 30 meters (nearly 100 feet) from the source, drilling may produce sound no louder than 85 dBA, riveting 80, and air compressor sound 75. And even this is forbidden from 7 A.M. to 7 P.M. While construction machinery exists that could meet these standards, much of the equipment, particularly in the smaller cities, is old and cannot even approach them. In addition, construction on the roads or the subway is exempted from the night laws, because heavy traffic limits daytime work. Traffic jams in the large cities are so formidable that an Osaka businessman with an appointment in Tokyo will leave for a nearby train station an hour ahead of train time. Drilling crews may also crack through the noise limit when work is needed because of disaster, to prevent "danger to human life or body," and to secure regular service of a railway.

"Because people suffer so much with nighttime road construction, the chief of the police department has unconditionally ruled that it should never be done on roads less than nine meters [about 30 feet] wide," stated Tomio Mochizuki, who is in charge of noise abatement for the Tokyo Research Institute.

This ruling keeps the drills and air compressors out of most residential districts at night, though they still disrupt the peace of city boulevards around entertainment and business districts.

The great cities of Japan have been torn apart by earthquakes in the past, and the danger remains. Building codes have specifications intended to prevent earthquake damage. Solid foundations, strong enough to withstand earth movements, are required for most buildings. The loudest part of construction, therefore, takes a long time. In Tokyo, noisiest of cities, there is an additional problem: the ground is very soft. In order for houses to stand firm, holes for foundations must be dug even deeper than elsewhere.

Some new building codes force abandonment of the Japanese traditional architecture, with vacant space between standing partitions and the pointed roof. Noise easily travels through that space. Room walls in new buildings must go all the way to the roof, which is less charming in style, but quieter than the old.

In highly industrialized Japan, the most extensive legislation naturally deals with factory noise. Each business enterprise must have staff members able to deal with pollution control. Noise limits are given for every conceivable type of machinery—shearing, forging, crushing, weaving, concrete- and asphalt-making, woodpulp grinding, plastic injection molding.

A businessman wanted to open a new factory. Before he could get a permit, he had to submit a report to the authorities reassuring them that the noise to be generated would be tolerable. Another factory owner decided to install a printing press. He had to apply for permission and describe how noisy the new machine would be.

"Noises much louder than those prescribed by law may be heard around factories," remarked Mr. Mochizuki of the Tokyo Research Institute. "If there are no victims of the noise, we let the factory be."

Neighbors of a factory in the city of Osaka complained. An inspector was sent to measure the noise level, and found that it exceeded the maximum. The manager received "administrative guidance," a recommendation for change. He did not respond, and so a definite order which could be enforced by law was given. Six factories in Osaka have received administrative guidance and two orders. Of these, six complied and the two others are working on improvements.

Cottage industries can be annoying, even when they follow the noise laws. "The trouble is that they are so close to houses," explained Noboru Nakasuji, senior noise officer, in Osaka City's Bureau of Public Health. "We can only have the parties concerned talk this over."

The situation is most acute at night when noise carries. "The small cottage industries try to work as many hours as possible."

Efforts to move factories into industrial zones or outlying districts have not been successful. The Japanese resist moving. Most people work for the same factory or company all their lives. "If you tell them to go, they will not," said Shiro Onishi director of Kyoto City's Public Hazards Office. "And everyone in an industry has to move from a residential area, or it is meaningless. The silk weaving business is in the middle of one of the residential areas of Kyoto. The porcelain potters live together, also. This is an old tradition. They have nostalgia. We have it, too. We and they feel if they move out from the old places, Kyoto is not Kyoto any more. Also the noise of weaving and the weaving machine symbolizes prosperity for them. They do not mind the noise. Even the younger generation does not want to move to new places. The Silk Weaving Institute of the Kyoto City government has devised a low-noise machine, and this is what the young people want, instead of moving.

"There has been some shifting out of the city, nonetheless. But the people who have moved are iron workers, not a traditional industry, just individuals scattered throughout Kyoto. So those who wanted to move got together. The city government purchases and prepares the land in an outlying district for use. Then the property is sold at a very cheap price to those people who are willing to move.

The price is much lower than an individual could find elsewhere."

A consultation day is held each week in the city of Osaka, another example of an imaginative approach to noise control. The management of any enterprise having a pollution problem can attend and seek advice from engineers of the municipal industrial research institute. Counselors will also visit a factory that is having noise problems.

The health centers in each municipal ward have environmental inspectors as staff members. When citizens come to the center to describe noisy situations, whether industrial or private, the inspectors will go out to check.

The municipal government of Kyoto, like most others in Japan, has a loan system to help small factories. A 10-year loan of 20 million yen at 5.5 percent interest is offered for moving, and a seven-year loan of 5 million yen at 1.8 percent for "reformation of facilities." In 1971, 41 loans were given and that was considered a bad year for Kyoto industry because of the first devaluation of the American dollar.

The Japanese system of loans and subsidies for pollution control is one of the most advanced and pragmatic approaches to the entire problem. Without such help the many small and undercapitalized firms in Japan could not insulate or improve equipment. When a businessman in Osaka applies to the city government for help, an official asks a commercial bank to extend a loan. The city then pays most of the interest. Should a factory wish to move from a residential to an industrial area, the city will buy the lots on which the business stands.

"Sometimes a factory cannot comply with the noise regulations, even with loan assistance," commented Mr. Nakatsuji, Osaka City's chief noise officer. "We could then order it to shut down. We have not resorted to that extreme case, as this touches on the right to operate a business and live."

Even the "Basic Law for Environmental Control" includes the provision that any action taken should be "adjusted to the sound economic growth of the national economy." The interests of industry have been running counter to those of environmentalists the world over.

In terms of enforcement there is considerable variation among cities and prefectures. But it is a regretable matter. Some factories have moved to other prefectures, because Osaka is too strict," remarked Takakazu Nakamura, in charge of noise control in the prefectural environmental agency.

Traffic noise is even harder to control than is industrial. The Japanese have had no more success than environmental officials elsewhere in inducing manufacturers to make quieter cars voluntarily. Noise limits for both old and new cars have now been set; however, the inspector examines a vehicle with regard to noise "by ear alone," calling for a sound meter only if he suspects it to be too loud.

"If cars on the streets are too noisy, the police can stop them and the drivers can be fined," said Takashi Shimodaira of the Motor Vehicles Department. "But not very many police are stopping cars for noise."

Little is done about traffic control, partly because the law, imaginative again, is so hard to enforce. The noise of all vehicles in a given area is considered as a whole, and can only be reduced by such drastic expedients as refusing trucks, buses, or cars the use of an entire zone. Some of these measures have been instituted on a limited basis. No cars are allowed on Sundays, for example, on the Ginza, Tokyo's commercial and entertainment section.

"But the problem is that the power to regulate traffic noise is in the hands of the police force, which is prefectural," said Mr. Onishi of the Kyoto city government. "The mayor does not have the power. The police are concerned with safety. If asked to do something about noise on a busy street, they say that they worry about accidents and do not care about the noise . . . and that is the trouble."

This was not always so. "Twenty years ago we were the first of the cities to say that the driver must not blow his horn. The reason why this law was kept by drivers so beautifully was that police headquarters were then under the city government. The shift to the prefecture was made in 1965. The same problem exists in all big cities."

Still, not only in Kyoto, but even in Tokyo and Osaka, horn-blowing is not as frequent as in American cities, even during traffic jams.

Motorcycles and unmuffled cars, however, are just as popular as in the United States. The noise made by motorcycles is theoretically regulated, yet in reality, officials concede, "the owner usually does as he wishes." At times citizens are maddened by the noise. In Toyama City motorcycles roared and car races went on through the streets all night. Newspapers and television programs carried a campaign against this and at last one night the police stepped in and arrests were made for breaking the speed limit. By this time a mob had grown and a panic resulted.

Traffic and industrial noise—hard to control as they are—do not compare with that produced by aircraft. The small size of the country and the large amount of trade and travel make the problem even more acute than elsewhere. Each year 147,000 planes, including 94,-000 jets, are flown to and from Tokyo's Haneda International Airport, and 124,000, with 49,000 jets, use Osaka's Itami International Airport. The decision to build a third international airport, Narita, just outside Tokyo was vehemently opposed by the public, but the demonstrations were ineffectual.

Civil Aviation officials in the Ministry of Transport blame much of the noise on the United States, because the jets in use are American-made. Yet despite this dependence, Japan has been able to make the regulations in Osaka the most stringent of those for any major international airport—and to enforce them. A cooperative council was set up by the II cities most affected by the noise from Itami Airport. A night curfew is so strict that it is broken by eight mail flights only. Should an airplane seek to land even one minute after 10:30 P.M., it is refused permission, and is forced on to Tokyo. Day and night are divided into four time periods, with specific noise limits set for each. Tokyo also has extremely strict laws, but officials admit that they find it impossible to enforce them.

"If international flights were refused the right to land at night at Tokyo as well as Osaka, the plane would have to go on to Taipei or Seoul," explained Kutaro Ishino of the Civil Aviation Bureau.

The necessity for enforcing Osaka's regulations at Tokyo's expense is explained by topography: Tokyo is bounded on three sides by the sea and Osaka is landlocked. "Osaka's stringent rules are the most necessary because housing is more condensed around the airport," said Kuniji Toda of the Ministry of Transport.

Efforts are being made to purchase houses near airports and then replace homes with factories. But they were unable, said officials, to buy up as much land around the new Narita Airport as would be desirable. If the noise level is above a specified maximum, subsidies are given to those who wish to move homes and factories. There are complaints, however, that nothing is done for people in areas where noise is too loud for comfort, but is not above the legal limit.

The government has been subsidizing soundproofing of public housing, schools, and hospitals near international airports. In 1972 the program was expanded to include some private homes. This is a "tremendous project," said Saburo Matsui, noise control chief of the national environmental agency, pointing to the 100,000 houses near Itami. The current plan is to contribute for quieting 30,000 homes there, 10,000 near the Haneda airport of Tokyo, and 4,000 at Narita. The cost for insulating a wooden house is about a million yen.

But despite all efforts to ameliorate its effects, aircraft noise has aroused the citizens of Japan to action. Even the Osaka laws are not held sufficient. School children in Kawanishi City near Itami were urged to write essays on how they feel about planes. "No tobanaide" (Don't Fly Any More) was the title of the book compiled from their writings. Several hundred households banded together to request a change of air routes.

The Sufferers' League has protested that citizens should have the right to tranquility, yet airplane noise often breaks into the "family get-together" hours. The league has made its own survey, which showed that noise might affect the fetus. It claimed the growth rate of infants near the airport to be inferior to that of children born to mothers in quieter areas. The league even attacked the system of buying individual lots near an airport so that people could relocate. The purchase prices for property are too low, and the government does not find any places for relocation.

Three cases, involving a total of 264 individuals, have been brought against the Ministry of Transport. The claim is that these people have suffered physical damage due to aircraft noise. They have sued for 500,000 yen to cover doctors' fees and ask the government to pay 19,000 yen per person a month until sound levels of 65 decibels or lower are produced at airports.

"There is no plane that can do that," commented aviation official Ishino. In his view, "The airport provides one of the major means of transport. As a citizen, one must compromise certain points."

The Civil Aviation Bureau dismisses the complaint of health damage: "It is a matter of worldwide opinion—present airplane noise has no serious physical effect and noise itself does not do great harm to health."

While research into the effects of noise is comparatively limited in Japan a number of scientists there take issue with that view. "I have interviewed people around the airport. I think they are nervous.

They are overanxious, very afraid for their children," declared Dr. Yasutaka Osada of the government's Institute of Public Health, who has headed a five-year study of 1,000 households in the noise zone around the Yokata United States military air base near Tokyo. Many residents complained of headache and ear pains, palpitation, and trouble sleeping.

Mr. Nakamura, in charge of Osaka's noise research, stated: "It is not definite, but probably noise pollution will affect little children who need fresh and keen vivid minds to accept tuition and learn music."

An environmental expert summed up the problem that has haunted those bringing suits—and not only in Japan: "If the evil effects of aircraft noise could be proved, then the people will win. So it depends on whether the doctors can prove this. If only the noisiness of aircraft is considered, then the people will not win, because planes are necessary."

Relief for noise sufferers may come as the result of a case dealing with a different form of pollution. In the summer of 1972 the citizens of Yokaichi won a lawsuit brought against 12 petrochemical companies accused of polluting the air. An illness aptly named "Yokaichi asthma" had become common and some people had died of it. The plaintiffs had not proved definitively that air pollution coming from a specific industrial plant caused the illness. The victory that was achieved was the first for such a case in Japan. It could serve as a precedent for the noise suits, and might encourage industries to observe the noise laws more closely without waiting to be sued.

Lawsuits represent only one aspect of a current revolt by Japanese citizens against noise. The national environmental agency received 22,568 complaints against noise and vibration in 1970, amounting to 35.6 percent of total complaints in that year. About 5,000 noise complaints are made yearly in Tokyo. In the city of Osaka alone, roughly 1,300 of 3,600 complaints made in an average year are about noise. "Residents of a compound of apartment buildings learned that the city is planning a nearby highway, which will increase traffic noise," said Mr. Nakatsuji. "They are appealing to the prefecture, and the public hazard examining commission is to determine whether the highway will be a nuisance."

One after the other, citizens' groups are forming.

"I started the movement because my house was in an industrial area with a number of very small factories. It was not only because I was a victim of noise pollution, but also because I wanted to do something good for society," said Mieko Baba, who described herself as an "ordinary Tokyo housewife." She is the founder of the "Tokyo metropolitan citizens to prevent noise pollution."

When started, the group was concerned with "privately-made" noises, such as practicing the piano or other musical instruments or excessive radio volume, but in time they raised broader issues. "We went to government officials to present concrete examples and through these examples to make the officials see how they could frame ordinances to control and give the needed correction," said Mrs. Baba, who found the reaction encouraging. "It always happens that the response is very weak when an individual appeals to a factory owner or government official. When you go in a group, people are more impressed and tend to listen. In that way we are a success."

Other citizens' groups include the 300-member Association of Victims of Noise Pollution, who engage in "enlightenment activities." Sixty families banded together in September, 1971, to appeal for reduction of subway construction din. Others are opposing factory noise. Another 2,000-member group was founded to fight against air pollution, but has now decided to battle noise, too. Nighttime noise is specifically opposed by a combination of 12 organizations.

The citizens' group By Our Own Hands, of Kyoto, takes up a different cause every year, and in 1968 the goal was "Let's make our quiet city." This program was so successful that people have been trying to follow the suggestions made ever since. "It was established in our minds very well."

Another movement in Kyoto, led mainly by women, has a name translated variously as the Association for Living Pollution Control or the Protection and Control from Living Pollution Association. The members study each problem, invite lecturers from universities to address them, and sometimes go to City Hall to complain. Said the men in the noise office: "They are very eager, very serious ladies."

Each year the number of complaints against noise begins to increase in May and June, reaches its peak in July and August, and declines in September and October. Officials explain that windows in factories and homes are kept open, and business goes on as usual during the hottest months. "People are more nervous in the summer. And we do not take vacations."

The Japanese culture is such as to make protest of any kind unusual. Acceptance, according to national tradition, is taken as a virtue. The average person has been trained to give way to superiors in business, to government officials. A strong sense of caste still exists. Arranged marriages, particularly among the wealthy, do take place, although marrying for love is more common than in the past. The position of women is secondary; liberation extends to very few. Many are limited to homes and children and do not join their husbands in the round of evening business entertainment. Job opportunities are poor. A handful of women, except for those filing or bringing tea, is seen in government offices.

Men work hard in their jobs and have little energy or time to concern themselves with outside events. They are only half-joking when they describe themselves as "economic animals." On weekdays employees are in the offices until late in the evening. The practice is so engrained that men working in the foreign department of one city government office say they are much envied. The chief spent some years abroad and became "westernized"; he goes home at 5:30 P.M. Elsewhere the director stays late and his subordinates do not feel it wise to leave before he does.

Yet individuals are forming groups, filing complaints, and bringing suits in this country where it runs counter to tradition. Women, discouraged from independent thought and activity, are taking the lead. The very fact that an outcry against noise can arise in Japan shows that the era when noise could be overlooked anywhere is over. And if environmental standards can be raised in Japan, they can be raised in countries where there is more land space and a long tradition of action by citizens.

Noise has accompanied industrialization and urbanization in Japan as it has elsewhere. The change that noise has brought to this Oriental country is evidence indeed of the way the quality of life can be affected and the sense of peace and tranquility destroyed.

As Mr. Onishi of Kyoto said: "A beautiful place with a beautiful culture should be quiet. People should be able to come to take pleasure in the quietness. We would like in the future to keep tourists from driving into this historic city. They should walk slowly and enjoy our beauty."

MAKING THE MACHINE 11
RUN QUIETLY

"THE MOST DEPLORABLE ASPECT *of existence in American cities may not be murder, rape, and robbery, but the constant exposure of children to pollutants, noise, ugliness, and garbage in the streets,"* Dr. *René Dubos, professor emeritus of Rockefeller University has written as foreword to a report on mental health.*

Is escape from the "constant exposure" possible? An engineer, under contract to the Environmental Protection Agency, traveled all over the country, recording the sounds that he heard. The quietest place he found was located just on the north rim of the Grand Canyon. For a short period each day noise levels were as low as 12 decibels. Even there, the stillness was broken from time to time by the passage of jet airplanes and small sightseeing craft. The average sound level heard at a farm in a valley was 44 dBA. But knowing that these out-of-the-way places can be peaceful is not really helpful to the average person, crowded with his fellows in the large cities. The engineer observed that the third floor of an apartment building next to a California freeway was the noisiest for a residential area. The median noise level was 88.8 dBA, with periodic peaks of greater sound.

"Men have founded civilization by exploiting natural resources . . . enjoying natural benefits. On the other hand, civilization has worked havoc upon nature. So it may be said that environmental pollution has its sources in industries and cities which man created and it obviously is a social calamity," wrote the Tokyo Metropolitan Research Institute for Environmental Protection.

Acoustical engineers insist that this calamity could be reversed. "The knowledge and technology exist now to control almost every indoor or outdoor noise problem," Dr. William W. Lang, manager of the acoustical laboratory of International Business Machines, declared at an American Association for the Advancement of Science meeting.

"There are solutions for quieting machines that are feasible and economically viable right now and that should be commonplace in the next ten years. In many cases nothing is needed beyond the simplest applications of theoretical acoustics with an understanding of how to build the hardware," stated acoustical engineer Lewis Goodfriend.

As proof that solutions exist, he pointed out that the equipment designed for the military had been quieted. Power generators, radar, and radios operate noiselessly. Even a teletype machine cannot be heard at a distance of six feet. The air conditioning within the Navy's nuclear submarines is virtually noiseless.

"Most of the designs used for military goods have been readily available for years. But the principles have not been applied to consumer products."

Appliances that make homes cooler and cleaner also make the idea that a home is a haven of peace seem curiously antiquated. An ordinary refrigerator produces sound of 45 decibels, an air conditioner 55, washing machine and clothes drier, 63 each, a dishwasher 68, and vacuum cleaner 73, reveals a recent appliance study carried out at the University of Wisconsin. A hair drier gives forth noise in decibels of 78, garbage disposal, electric can opener, and knife sharpener of 79 each, an electric mixer 82, shaver 85, exhaust fan 90, and blender 92. And this is when each one is being used separately, which seldom occurs in the home.

Dr. Lee E. Farr of the University of Texas Graduate School of the Biomedical Sciences has measured what happens when only a few are run simultaneously. Starting in the living room of a typical apartment in Houston, he noted a background noise level of 50 decibels, which was quite acceptable. Then the vacuum cleaner was plugged in, and when the nozzle was lifted to go over the upholstery, the hum reached 81 decibels. This was the same as the sound pro-duced by the high-fidelity set, heard from a chair six feet away from the speakers. That, to be sure, was viewed by the family as music not noise. In the kitchen of the apartment he found the greatest number of sound assaults. The air conditioner and the vent fan over the stove produced a noise level of 84 decibels. When the dishwasher was turned on, the total kitchen noise rose to 88, and adding the garbage disposal unit brought it to 100 decibels.

Certainly, no one runs all appliances all the time. Yet the person leading what is still called the quiet life at home is exposed daily to sound sufficient to damage hearing if it were continued for long enough. Even brief periods of appliance use interrupt speech and break into thoughts, adding to the tension and fatigue of housework. The University of Wisconsin researchers have urged an appliance noise limit of 70 decibels.

The household could be run quietly, but it is not—largely because far from demanding quiet appliances, the public asks for noisy ones. This demand, illogical in the face of the all-but-universal longing for a quiet home environment, is a carryover from the time when appliances were newly invented, and compared to today, crudely designed. Interviews (conducted for the Environmental Protection Agency) with three manufacturers and one retailer of vacuum cleaners disclosed that each was convinced "customers use noise as the basis for judging the power of a machine." Though that once was true, it no longer applies to the majority of home appliances. One manufacturer said that he had cut down the noise in one of his canister models. When this machine was given a market test, housewives repeatedly asked if the vacuum were really picking up the dirt.

The maker of a power mower succeeded in reducing the noise level of his most popular model, and many were sold. What was the result?

"They began to be returned because they were 'underpowered,' " reported Cecil R. Sparks of the applied physics department, Southwest Research Institute, at a public hearing.

Of four washing machine manufacturers questioned, two made quiet models selling for $10 to $20 more than the standard models. Sales of these were found to be disappointing. This may be why a search of mail-order catalogs found "quiet" in the description of only one washing machine.

None of the manufacturers interviewed intended to give up his noisier economy line. Appliances have for years, like automobiles, been designed for power and the added noise has been ignored. When the speed of the spinner in the washing machine was increased, so was the noise. Producers point out that they are expected to keep on bringing out new models that can do more than earlier ones. Refrigerators, once noisy, became silent; then ice-makers and frost-free freezers were added. A blender could be made quieter if it were slowed down, say manufacturers, but then it would not be as efficient. One of the few relatively quiet hair driers has been found to take many minutes longer to dry hair than do some of the noisier models.

Making the machine run quietly **113**

Although these examples are often presented by appliance makers, a number of acoustical engineers view them as excuses, and no more. Mr. Goodfriend, for example, declares: "You can muffle a machine and have no loss in efficiency."

When losses occur—and they obviously do—they are thus attributed to poor acoustical or engineering techniques, the concern for economy, or the stultifying effect of the desire to maintain the status quo. Manufacturers lack the incentive to produce quieter models. Most regulations deal with heavy industrial machinery and appliances are ignored.

The technology required to reduce appliance noise is not necessarily complicated, engineers point out. Engines or parts of them can be enclosed in soundproofed materials. The tub of a dishwasher might be wrapped in glass fiber and a shield of similar material built in to reduce garbage disposal noise. The motor of a vacuum cleaner could be suspended within the tank, one designer has suggested, the discharge pipe redirected into the machine, and the hose treated with soundproofing materials. The vibration produced by washing machines, electric coffee mills, and a host of other appliances could be absorbed by mounting on soft rubber. The window air conditioner is particularly annoying, because it consists of a vibrating source attached to a sounding board. If the conditioner were mounted on resilient brackets, the vibration would be minimized. Substitutes can be found for materials that make a lot of noise when they hit or rub against one another. Plastic beaters on mixers are quieter than metal, for example. The shape of a machine also affects the amount and kind of noise it produces. Certain blade configurations for fans avoid the most annoying of the frequencies produced by the whirring. Engineers at one appliance laboratory are working on an ice crusher to make a "growling" rather than a raucous sound.

What does noise reduction do to the cost of an appliance? A manufacturer had some gears taken out of a washing machine as an economy measure. In an unplanned side-effect, the washer became quieter. This result is so unusual that the story has become legendary. As a rule, quiet machinery and appliances cost more than noisy ones, though there is no agreement on just how much more. One dishwasher manufacturer has estimated that the price would rise $10 if the dishwasher were made quieter than it is now, and $20 if it were altered to be almost noiseless. Another has calculated an increase of 10 percent in production costs for quieting a machine, while a third thought it would add only $1 to $2 at the manufacturing level. A disposal manufacturer has figured that an addition of 12 percent would be needed. There have been estimates that a quieter air conditioner would cost from 10 to 15 percent more and might be bigger and less attractive. (Some people have suggested putting the noisy part of the conditioner outside the window, thus shifting the problem from the individual to the community.)

Whatever the added initial cost, however, incorporating quieting features in a machine is usually cheaper than adding a gadget, installing acoustic material, or building an enclosure later. Vibration not only causes noise, but shakes a machine and shortens its life. Controlling this from the start would be economical in the long run.

Cost could be held down from the very beginning by mass production. The key difficulty gets back to the lack of consumer demand. Not only do buyers fail to insist on quieter machines when they go out shopping, but their objections to the ones they have are made to spouses and friends, not manufacturers. The industry's Major Appliance Consumer Action Panel has noted that only five percent of letters of complaint received in the first eight months of 1971 concerned noise. Such complaints are most often about air-conditioners. Of the smaller appliances, fans, mixers, and hair driers are mentioned. A vacuum cleaner manufacturer who regularly analyzes customer complaints told the Environmental Protection Agency that noise is hardly ever brought up.

Making the machine run quietly **115**

The very individuals who complain vehemently to government agencies about traffic, aircraft, construction, and neighbors' noises remain silent about the appliances they bring into their homes. And these present a source which the consumer could control to a considerable extent—if only he knew it.

The lack of both complaint and demand can be blamed almost entirely on lack of information. There have been few efforts to explain to homemakers that noise is not invariably a sign of power in a machine. Yet advertising and publicity campaigns have put across far more complex ideas.

At present, freedom of choice does not exist. Even those who want quieter equipment are hard-pressed to find it, or to recognize it when they do. Despite the concern expressed by manufacturers about the added cost of noise reduction, the highest-priced appliance is not necessarily the quietest. Customers are expected, and encouraged by advertising, to pay extra for color, shape, or special features that are not essential.

One careful purchaser asks salesmen to turn on machines in the store. "They can seldom find any outlets within easy reach. And even when the machine is run for me, the way it sounds on the floor or display table of a large department store is very different from the noise it produces at home in my basement or on my kitchen table."

Consumer goods, as well as industrial products, should be noise-tested, and then clearly noise-labeled.

The techniques and materials that could or do quiet home appliances have in many instances been developed for heavy, industrial machinery. Efforts to quiet the factory environment go back through the years, while that of the home is neglected. Many industrial plants today shroud machines or their noisiest components in soundproofed material or place them in soundproofed enclosures. Acoustical panels suspended from the ceiling, mounted on the walls, or set up as screens also are used to keep sound from passing to another room or part of a room. The noise from rooftop ventilators over a Chicago paint store irritated the neighbors until the owner had a shield built around them. Acoustical material is incorporated in some equipment. Compressed polyurethane foam, for example, reduced the 80-decibel noise level of a computer system to 55 decibels.

Vibration is a far greater problem for heavy machinery than for the home appliance, but the principle of mounting on resilient material works for both.

A gas turbine generating system produced a low-pitched rumble that shook windows and rattled doors. The rumble was not at an audible frequency, so the discomfort was blamed on vibration alone.

"Using fundamental theory," remarked Mr. Goodfriend, "we saw the trouble and installed a muffler. And nothing rattles any more."

Noise can be controlled in two ways: at the source or by changing the path between the source and the listener, explained Dr. Lang of I.B.M.

Noisy equipment can be positioned so that the sound waves travel in a direction away from workers or residents of nearby homes. In Chicago a complaint was served against the owner of a clattering air conditioner. Common sense should have told him to place the conditioner in a spot where it did not face a neighboring house, but this was not done until he got into trouble. Often, the noisiest equipment can be placed in the basement of factory, apartment building, or school.

If a person moves away from a noise source—as he will certainly do if possible—each time the distance from it doubles, the sound he hears is reduced by six decibels.

Fighting noise with "anti-noise," an original approach utilizing the relative positions of noise producer and listener, has been described in an article by Charles J. Lynch, associate editor of *International Science & Technology*. As its name implies, anti-noise is the mirror image or opposite frequency of the original noise. It is created electronically and sent out to meet the noise coming in to the ear of the listener. The two sounds then cancel one another out. Should either the noise, anti-noise, or listener shift position, however, then the two noises would reinforce one another. The method is most successful in controlling the kind of steady low-frequency hum given out by some motors. The wavelength of such sounds is long enough to allow slight movement by the listener. Anti-noise has limited usefulness, because it does not work well with high-frequency sound, or more important, with the mixed frequencies which make up most noises.

An observant factory worker complained that white noise had been installed as an alternative to quieting the machines. The owner of an office building with noisy, antiquated elevators had music piped in to drown out the clanking of chains and pulleys.

A number of the techniques that are supposed to make people oblivious to machinery noise are offensive; many become livid about having to listen to "Some Enchanted Evening" while in the elevator going to the dentist's office. These devices can also represent an inefficient and sometimes unnecessarily costly substitute for redesigning the equipment itself. That is done only when public clamor is great enough. Complaints about garbage trucks breaking the pre-dawn quiet of the streets mounted until officials in one city responded by refusing to place any more orders for the noisiest models. Garbage trucks were then redesigned and, though still far from silent, became 60 percent quieter than before. The additional expense was $120 apiece.

Part of the cost of quieting machines and appliances lies in the investment that must be made by the manufacturer for research and design. More than 10,000 engineering design hours were needed to work out a way of reducing the sound of a tractor at the operator's station by seven decibels, declared Jack Hasten, manager of the products control department of the Caterpillar Tractor Company, at an Environmental Protection Agency hearing.

Such efforts are not always hailed by the men who must operate construction equipment in quarries. They complain that it is harder to judge the pace of the loading with a muffled engine. Many also like "the feeling of power" gained from racing the engine loudly as they pull away from the crusher.

The need for building often runs counter to the need for quiet, and the plight of neighbors is coolly overlooked. For some months the residents of an apartment house in Queens, New York, waited impatiently for nightfall to bring them release from the nerve-shattering din produced by construction of a bridge leading into New York City. On one occasion, however, the noise continued until midnight. The builders had run behind schedule and were trying to catch up by working extra shifts. The nearby tenants could not talk in normal tones, or listen to television, or rest, even with windows closed. At last they decided to go to court. Recordings made inside the rooms were introduced as evidence, and the judge ruled that construction be discontinued at night.

Since that time the noise code passed in New York City prohibits construction at night. To be sure, city historians recall that New York had a noise code in 1936, which had long ago been amended to include a similar ban on nighttime construction. There were a host of other prohibitions, as on noise from animals and birds. But most provisions of that code were not enforced. Have times changed? A woman recently complained that "dog noise" is the worst of all. Her neighbors' dogs bark day and night, and no one takes her complaints seriously. The captain of one New York City police department precinct, reported Citizens for a Quieter City, has ordered his patrolmen to give summonses to men drivers sounding their horns so as to get the attention of prostitutes on the sidewalk. No comment was made on whether this has contributed to an overall decline in horn-blowing.

Five summonses, each with a threatened fine of a thousand dollars, have been served on a construction company working most of the night on a Manhattan apartment house. Nearby residents are awakened reguarly. The company, however, was undeterred by the summonses, as it would cost far more than fines to be late in finishing the job.

Large portable air compressors are known to make the most objectionable noise during in-city construction. Eight or nine are frequently lined up along a curb near an apartment building. Each produces sound of 110 to 112 dBA, measured at a distance of one meter. This is twice as loud as a subway train pulling into a station. In addition, the sound is reflected back and forth between machines and buildings.

Ingersoll-Rand Company has reduced the noise of an air compressor to about 85 dBA, which is roughly 18 percent of the original level. "We call it 'whisperized,' " said George M. Diehl, sound and vibration consultant.

Machines will ultimately be even quieter. An experimental unit that produces only 73.5 dBA has already been displayed.

It has been hard to persuade the construction companies to buy the quieter equipment that is now available. When New York City's Commissioner of Air Resources wrote to 700 construction companies asking about their noise-abatement practices, he received only four answers. It is not that the other 696 like to be shunned as noise-makers, but they prefer it to spending extra money. A crawler drill treated to produce 100 instead of 120 decibels of sound costs 10 to 15 percent more. Were manufacturers to bring the noise down to 90 decibels, the price would rise by about 30 to 40 percent. The cost of a large diesel-engine compressor is increased nearly a third by noise control.

What contractor would pay these prices when he could be underbid for a job by another using less quiet machines?

"Originally all manufacturers insisted they would be bankrupt if required to meet standards," said acoustical expert Goodfriend. "When yardsticks were set for air compressors in New York City, for example, these were said to be impossible in a business sense. But if every contractor were required to use quiet compressors, then it becomes possible for all."

"For a long time we worked intermittently on muffling paving breakers. There is no measurable loss of impact power. But no one wanted them," declared Mr. Diehl. "Now they do."

A gradual reduction in construction machinery sound levels over the next few years is required by law. The quiet equipment once used by the few will become the standard. Perhaps in time even this exceptional construction story will become commonplace: Several years have passed since a 52-story building was put up in the business district of New York. The joints of the building were welded, so as to eliminate riveting altogether. Steel wire mesh blankets were spread over the site to muffle the sound of blasting. The loudest sound heard during the construction by people working across the street was the warning beep.

PROTECTING THE HOME 12

"IF I WERE *to open the window, you would soon find yourself shouting,"* said a tenant in an apartment building near a busy highway. *"I see a moving van in front of the building almost every day."*

Residents of houses set back from a highway are disturbed, too. Noise levels of 75 to 80 decibels will drown out the television in homes 100 feet away. A quiet evening is not possible even for those living at a 1,000-foot distance, with sound of 60 to 65 decibels reaching the home.

Housing projects that would place thousands of people directly under the airplane approach and takeoff paths to two busy airports were cited by Franklin Kolk, a vice-president of American Airlines. "If these were isolated instances, they would be understandable or forgivable," he told the Environmental Protection Agency, "but they happen all too frequently, all over the country."

Seven and a half million people, at the lowest estimate, are housed on the 1,500 square miles that encircle existing airports, and several times that number live close enough to be disturbed regularly by jet noise.

Efforts to make up for housing mistakes of the past are rare—and costly. The city of Los Angeles recently spent $97,000 to buy a house on the outskirts of Los Angeles International Airport. The next bill paid was $360 to have the house demolished. This was part of a project to buy up the 2,560 homes in the 600-acre area around the airport at a cost of more than $108 million. Reports circulated of prices of $28,000 . . . $115,000 . . . paid for a single house. Those that were resold for moving to another location brought from $300 to $3,000.

As the result of court action, the airport authority has also been required to soundproof some, and build other, well-insulated schools.

Expensive errors like these could be avoided in the future if private builders met the noise standards required by the Department of Housing and Urban Development for all its projects. A new construction site is rated by the government as unacceptable if the outside noise level exceeds 80 dBA for 60 minutes of the day and night, or 75 dBA for eight hours. Special permission from the regional administrator is required for housing in places where noise is greater than 65 dBA for eight hours. During the traditional sleeping hours, sound inside the house is not to exceed 45 dBA for longer than a total of 30 minutes. Insulation between dwelling units as well as between the house and the outside is also required. But rumors persist that these regulations are not always followed. Where public housing is badly enough needed, it may be put up despite some drawbacks. Still, the Department has made a start.

A Minneapolis family wanted to buy a frame house located about 125 feet away from a highway, and applied for government financing. A government inspector came to check, and he then refused to recommend the loan. The house was classed as unacceptable, because of "excessive noise from the highway." The prospective buyer wrote to the Department of Housing and Urban Development to point out that as the mother of five children, she was used to noise. The agency would not budge.

It has also rejected two projects for low- to middle-income housing viewed as being too close to an airport.

After one low-income housing project was turned down on grounds of traffic noise, a letter appeared in the local newspaper, citing the desperate need for housing and commenting that it had taken 12 years for the required appropriation to be approved. This letter presented the commonly held view that noise reduction cannot be achieved without the sacrifice of something else. But must something else be sacrificed? When contracts for building are given out, construction requirements are made, but hardly ever are American architects forced to take noise into account. Soundproofing thus is considered sheer luxury—often too much of a luxury for high-rent buildings, too—until the recent government actions.

Noise levels can be written into building codes. This has been customary in England for many years. Similarly, maximum noise levels are part of housing regulations in the Netherlands, Sweden, Germany, the U.S.S.R., and many other countries. But relatively few cities in the United States have a code dealing with noise in any definitive way.

"It is a fact that there are more than 12,000 different building codes throughout the United States. Each of these could be interpreted as requiring some degree of airborne and structure-borne noise control," Alvin G. Greenwald, Los Angeles lawyer, has commented privately.

Even when, as in New York City, demands are made, the standards are not easy to follow. They tell what noise in a room or building should be, and fail to specify which materials must be used to achieve this quiet. Not every contractor can translate an overall noise requirement into the exact wood and plastic he should buy. Manuals explaining such matters are readily available, but the excessive noise in many new buildings stands as proof that these go either unread or are ignored.

"One of the problems is that unless written into the contract, the acoustical consultant's charge comes out of the architect's fee," said Columbia University's Cyril Harris. "It should be made a separate item."

Building techniques to keep out noise have as a rule been applied only when apartments, offices, hospitals, or schools were built in areas obviously unsuitable for them. Tufts-New England Medical Center in Boston is surrounded by streets with heavy traffic and stands over subway tracks. Pads, two inches thick, made of layers of sheet lead, asbestos felt, and steel have been placed under the columns and around the base of the building to absorb the noise and vibration.

An even greater challenge was successfully met by builders of an elementary school only a mile away from the end of a runway at Kennedy International Airport, a site so noisy that even the Federal Aviation Administration strongly advised against its use. Yet the land was purchased, because it was reasonable in price, and architect Douglas J. Persich worked throughout with sound consultant Michael J. Kodaras. The building was air-conditioned, and the few windows were set in thick aluminum frames sealed with rubber gaskets. Floor slabs were of two-and-a-half-inch concrete, and four-to eight-inch-thick interior partitions kept the noise from passing between classrooms. Ceilings were suspended on spring hangers from the five-inch-thick concrete roof slab. Air space was left within the exterior walls, which were covered on the outside with blue brick and concrete.

In some states quiet for students has become a legal requirement. Schools in Hawaii must be insulated to protect youngsters from transportation noise. California, faced with an existing vast system of freeways, has ruled that no new roads may be built in areas near schools unless these are soundproofed.

The noise in Elizabeth, New Jersey, classrooms had averaged 60 decibels before new highways were built. The level then rose to 80 decibels. The city's Board of Education went to court, and with noise-measurement data as evidence, won its case. An award of $164,119 was given to cover the cost of sealing windows and air-conditioning the schools.

In sharp contrast, the kind of construction used by most home builders nowadays shuts out 15 to 20 decibels of exterior noise, according to a National Association of Home Builders manual.

Not only household appliances, but also houses and apartments might be noise-rated to the benefit of the buyer or renter, James L. Hildebrand wrote in the *Columbia Law Review*.

The individual, like the project planners, should consider noise when selecting a building site. One prospective buyer bought a sound-level meter and carried it to all the places he was considering. By 1972 the desire for these devices had reached the point where *New York* magazine, always alert to city buying trends, featured a $75 model, and described its journeyings through the city. When the bearer of the device stood on the subway platform, the needle jumped as high as the meter could register.

Noise detection of a potential home site can be done with no equipment, besides a tape measure, but a companion is essential. Two people, each holding one end of a tape measure, stand at the spot where the house is to be built or is now standing. One speaks, while the other starts walking away, unrolling the tape. Eventually, the listener cannot understand the speaker. If that happens at a distance of 25 feet or less, the area is obviously too noisy for comfortable living. Seventy feet or more approaches the ideal.

The home-builder should consider noise when drawing up a floor plan, and locate bedrooms as far away as possible from highways, restaurants, bars, nightclubs, and movie theaters. An acoustical engineer measured sound in the front and then the back rooms of a townhouse. The difference between the two levels was 20 dBA.

The principles of soundproofing applied to the elementary school near the airport can be used by the home-builder or buyer, too. "The two things to keep in mind are the openings to the outside and the thickness of outer wall and roof," an expert at Housing and Urban Development explained.

One buyer of a home in a modern development provided himself with the soundproofing the builder had neglected. He replaced the thin glass windows with double panes of glass. The most important aspect of the double window is the air space between the panes. The greater it is, the more sound it absorbs. Recognizing that noise can easily slip in through a thin wooden door, he substituted one made of a heavy solid block of wood. A double door, like a double window, would also be effective in holding back unwanted sound. Determined to achieve quiet, this buyer strengthed the outside of the frame house. Considerable protection is achieved by thickening exterior walls with soundproofing material, or even ordinary bricks or masonry.

Poor workmanship leaves room for noise to creep in. Cracks can appear even before a building is finished. If a space or hole is big enough for an ant to get through, it is big enough for noise to get through, a Bolt, Berenek and Newman promotional pamphlet has warned. One foreman commented that after a building is finished, he goes around it with a caulking gun making up for any deficiencies. As time goes by, cracks appear as a part of the aging process. A crack that is a mere 0.011 inches, but runs along the base of a 100-square-foot wall, produces an opening that is 1.4 inches square. Weatherstripping regular windows and doors helps keep noise as well as snow and rain outside.

The most effectively soundproofed building contains walls and floors that are heavy, but not stiff. It is even better if the flooring is suspended on resilient material and the insulation is placed within the cavities of walls.

Most people today show a marked lack of enthusiasm for the extra cleaning required by the waste space that characterized homes of the past. Halls, stairways, foyers, pantries, and attics have disappeared in response to this demand for convenience, which happens to coincide with high building costs and lack of land space in residential areas. It may have made work, but all this waste space served to prevent the encroachment of noise into the main living rooms. An attic, for example, by providing air space between roof and ceiling, helped to keep overhead noises from intruding.

Within a room, the longer it takes soundwaves to bounce from the walls, the louder and more troublesome they seem. When the waves come back within 0.3 to 0.7 second, then the background level is comfortable, and it is easy to talk and keep track of what is being said on the radio or television.

A young couple went into their new still unfurnished apartment and were horrified at how shrill and unpleasant their conversation and laughter sounded. The hardwood floor and gypsum board walls and ceilings had slowed the reverberation time to 1.4 seconds.

The amount of sound to hit the walls and bounce back can be controlled to some extent by furnishing. The medieval castle was sparsely furnished, considering its size, but tapestries were hung on the walls to keep out the cold. These also reduced the reverberation from the clank of armored feet on stone, the shouts of the knights, and the songs of the troubadours.

The modern-day couple decided on a bright, uncluttered style of decoration. They threw down a few brilliantly colored scatter rugs, and put up transparent drapes that would not keep out the light. Furnishings of plastic and chrome had stark and simple lines. The effect was dramatic, but of very little use in absorbing sound. When they visited their neighbors one night they noticed that the apartment, identical in plan to theirs, was quieter by far. There was wall-to-wall carpeting, and heavy drapes which were kept open by day for light and closed at night for sound absorption. Upholstered furniture with thick cushions took in a good part of the sound and prevented it from reverberating.

The materials selected by the builder also make the difference between a quiet and a noise-wracked interior. Not only gypsum and hardwood flooring, but also unglazed brick, linoleum, asphalt, and vinyl floor tiles have poor sound absorption. Coarse concrete block is good at taking in noise, while painted concrete is not. Plywood paneling, if at least three-eighths of an inch thick, is considerably more absorbent than plain gypsum board, or brick, but is not as effective as acoustical tile or sheets.

When interviewed on a television interview show, a doctor on the staff of a hospital commented that the noise level was so high that he had trouble hearing a patient's heartbeat and other chest sounds. A special problem exists at hospitals, because porous acoustical materials can absorb microorganisms along with the noise.

"At Columbia University's health service in St. Luke's Hospital, we have installed a polyvinyl sheet of acoustical tile that can be wiped off easily," said Dr. Harris. And he pointed out that much hospital noise comes from sources that could have been controlled by better planning. "Equipment and pumps have not been properly isolated."

The sound of plumbing in the next apartment, or reverberating through the house, is one of the most annoying of noise intrusions, because it underscores the lack of privacy. Reducing the water pressure will cut down on the noise, but this approach is for obvious reasons feasible only in buildings of three stories or fewer. In high-rise dwellings a series of pressure-regulating valves is needed at different levels. When a faucet is turned and only partially opens the valve, a high-pitched noise is produced that travels a long way through the pipes. Sound-absorbing materials can be wrapped around pipes or the holes through which they pass.

"No standards exist in the United States at present for measuring or rating the 'noisiness' of household faucets," complained the National Association of Home Builders manual.

The remark that was used as the title of a Broadway play, "you know I can't hear you when the water's running," has been tested in a suburban residential area in Austin, Texas. During the summertime when windows were open, background noise inside a home was usually 52 decibels. The rushing water of the shower raised the level to 82 decibels. Merely opening the faucets and letting the water run into the washbasin produced noise of 72 decibels. In the winter when some windows were closed and the background noise was held to 43 decibels, the sound of the central heating brought it up to 65 to 75 decibels. (The range covers the variety of brands used in that community.)

The growing resentment of the intrusion of noise is at last being reflected in home purchases. Some houses in a development in Birmingham, Alabama, were sound conditioned, while others were built in the standard manner with thin walls, unmuffled plumbing, and noisy air conditioning. The quieter homes cost from $600 to $800 more than the others, but they were the ones that sold first.

Builders and real estate brokers who once could sell virtually anything to house-hungry Americans are learning that prices of homes near airports must be reduced to sums far below any they could command elsewhere. Or they must be very well soundproofed. And even then, sales of such houses come slowly.

Homes near major highways are also avoided by buyers when possible. One summer a part of an expressway was being repaired and cars and trucks were detoured. People living in houses adjacent to the road said it was the best summer they could remember. "If only the thruway could be repaired all the time!"

AN IMMENSITY OF SOUND 13

"THE NOISE... *endowed by the horse . . . surged like a mighty heartbeat in the central districts of London's life. It was a thing beyond all imaginings . . . streets paved in granite . . . and the hammering of a multitude of ironshod heavy heels. . . . It was not any such paltry thing as noise. It was an immensity of sound."*

The "multitude of horses," so described in a British publication of the 1890s, is gone from the city streets, but noise is not. The sound of hooves on pavement has merely been replaced by tire screech and motor noise.

And the cities are ringed with mile upon mile of expressways. More than 265,000 vehicles travel Chicago's Kennedy Expressway in a single day, producing noise and air pollution. Estimates also put 226,000 cars a day on Los Angeles' Santa Monica Freeway, 178,000 on Detroit's Ford Freeway, and 159,000 on New York's Long Island Expressway.

Objections to road traffic noise were expressed by roughly half of all those surveyed by TRACOR in Chicago, Minneapolis, Saint

Paul, Denver, Los Angeles, Dallas, Miami, and New York.

Major changes in automotive design are now being demanded. While relief of air pollution is the primary goal, relief of noise pollution is being considered, too. Some people go so far as to urge giving up on the internal-combustion engine altogether and replacing it with an electric motor, steam engine, or gas turbine. A substitution of any of those would reduce both noise and air pollution at one blow, but none can as yet compete with conventional engines. They are not practical for mass use.

Even so, no one seriously questions the existence of technology right now capable of reducing the noise produced by the internal-combustion engine to levels well below those required in such noise codes as New York City's: 88dBA for trucks going at a speed of 35 miles or less per hour, measured at 50 feet, and 82 dBA for automobiles.

The government has been supporting engineering research to create a quieter truck engine. The emphasis on trucks stems from a Department of Transportation study suggesting that three trucks and 17 automobiles produce the same median sound level as 100 automobiles.

"Consider how different life would be for people with homes near highways, if truck noise could be brought down to the current goal of 75 to 78 dBA. Even this would not make it possible to play the television softly, but it would be a step in that direction," said an automotive engineer. "It is frustrating to realize that a truck engine quieter than that has already been developed. Known as the 'Golden Boy,' it simply has not proven practical to date."

Old-timers recall that when cars first went chug-chugging down the road, small boys would shout, "Get a horse." Today those hearing the trucks go by tend to rephrase that as "Get a muffler." Many people think that improving exhaust mufflers would solve the truck noise problem; that is only a beginning. The noise made by trucks would drop by a mere one-half a decibel at highway speeds and by three decibels at city limits were all exhaust noise completely eliminated, said William H. Close, who heads noise abatement research for the Department of Transportation. To do better than that means dealing with intake and fan noise, placing sound barriers around engine and transmission, and putting on tires less noisy than those commonly used today.

Driving fast gives some people a sense of power that goes to their heads. It also goes to their ears and those of other drivers, pedestrians, and residents of houses near the road. Current laws pragmatically allow an additional two dBA when vehicles go at speeds greater than 35 miles per hour. The faster the car goes, the more likely it is to have an accident. The faster the car goes, the more noise it must make. Low speed limits can do as much as mufflers, or as redesigning the engine, to reduce traffic noise. Drivers should emulate the tortoise, rather than the hare.

It has long been considered axiomatic that the driver longs for higher rather than lower speed limits, but this may be a misconception. Physics students at Drexel University had an assignment to conduct interviews on reactions to the lower speed limits imposed late in 1973. The purpose was to save fuel, but side-effects were savings in lives and in noise production. The number of traffic deaths fell by 1,200 a month when the lower speed limits were imposed. To the surprise of the interviewers, about half of all the men questioned did not oppose the lower limits. Even among those who drive for a living, universal support for speed could not be obtained. Two of five were in favor of going more slowly.

In order to encourage this attitude, a huge thermometer has been put up by the side of a busy highway in Edmonton, Alberta. Despite its appearance, it has nothing to do with the weather. The marker, stimulated by a microphone, responds to the sound of an approaching car. It shoots up showing the driver whether his noise tempera-

An immensity of sound **133**

ture is normal, thus within legal limits, higher, or rarely, lower. In this way, Canadian authorities have dramatized the need for compliance with the law.

The potential for automotive annoyance was recognized more than half a century before anything was done about it: "The invention of the automobile has introduced upon the public roads of the country a novel and not altogether welcome guest," wrote retired United States Supreme Court Justice H. B. Brown in 1908. "To those who occupy or drive them, they are undoubtedly a fascinating amusement," but he commented on the "arrogant disregard" of others. Even then, he saw the solution as clear: "A few sharp lessons from the courts may inculcate more respect for the rights of others."

The courts and legislatures were slow to give such lessons. The first federal law to consider national standards for vehicle noise was the Noise Control Act of 1972. Under the provisions of this law, the limits are to be set for the manufacturer; the goal is to make trucks as quiet as cars by 1983. States also set limits for traffic noise.

State laws antedate the federal law, but not by much. No rush to "inculcate more respect for the rights of others" followed Justice Brown's observation. New York was the first state to limit actual vehicle noise, and this did not happen until October 1, 1965. The law neglected to set standards for cars driven faster than 35 miles per hour and did not order the manufacturers to make quieter vehicles. California's law, passed a year later, was remarkable as the first to give a complete list of maximum sound levels for cars and trucks, depending on age. California looked to the future and demanded that, with the passing years, vehicles be designed for ever greater quiet. Reductions were spelled out to a 1980 goal of comparative silence.

By the end of 1971, 43 states in the United States had laws requiring mufflers on cars, and 15 had ordinances against horn-blowing.

Only a few limited actual vehicle noise, following the lead of New York and California.

Snowmobiles and "leisure time" vehicles also must meet test standards in a number of states. The snowmobiles of 79 manufacturers were checked for noise in New York, and those made by 49 of the producers failed the test. These manufacturers were forbidden to offer their 1973 models for sale in the state until they had brought down the noise. In Massachusetts and Vermont the snowmobile limit has been set at 82 decibels.

The need for such regulation becomes apparent with sales, the Forest Service reports, reaching the one-half-million-units a year rate. "Snowmobile before college," wrote the *New York Times*. One reason for an enrollment decline was suggested by the treasurer of a prestigious New England college: "People make choices—a second car, a snowmobile—versus private college."

Legislative demands for change in snowmobiles, trucks, and cars coming off the production line will help but not eliminate the traffic noise problem. Like all things animate and inanimate, vehicles fall apart in old age. Parts that originally fit perfectly begin to clank and rattle. Many modern trucks are well made and equipped with mufflers that really do what they should. Then these wear out and more often than not, replacements are inferior in fit, design, and materials. Proper maintenance can overcome many failings of vehicular old age, but a good number of owners do just enough to keep the car or truck running and to barely get it past an inspection. An effective law, therefore, should require any vehicle on the road to meet a given noise limit, not only when new, but for its entire driving life.

Traffic noise laws are vigorously enforced by some states and cities, not by others. California is so strict about this that 18,000 tickets were given out in 1971. And this was done by only six two-man teams of patrolmen assigned to check the state's 162,000 miles of highway. Police in Memphis are issued portable decibel meters to measure noise on the streets and roads in and around the city. Three times a year every vehicle must be brought in for inspection. On the other hand, in New York, where more than 1,000 trucks per hour go down the Thruway, only six summonses for noise violations were given in 1968 and 1969.

A number of states, cities, and countries abroad have set stringent noise standards; others are much more relaxed. While South Africa and Switzerland might seem to have little in common, both, as of December, 1971, had a 79-decibel limit for heavy trucks traveling at highway cruising speeds, as heard by someone 50 feet away. The maximum noise level allowed by law in the United Kingdom at that time was 86 decibels and in the Netherlands it was 88, reported Dr. Schultz of Bolt Berenek and Newman.

West Germany was the first of the Common Market countries to set noise limits for traffic, and with minor changes its code has been adopted by the rest. The noise produced by vehicles must correspond to the level that can be achieved in accordance with the "current state of the art." It sounds reasonable, but when control of pollution is involved, the state of the art of technology tends to fluctuate wildly, depending on the desire for economy, industrial pressures, and official interest. The health minister in 1966 showed what he thought of this carefully worded ruling by urging engineers to aim at going beyond the state of the art.

The Organization for Economic Cooperation and Development has been conducting a program among its 23 member nations to encourage the institution of traffic-noise-reduction programs.

The Nordic Committee for Building Regulations (Nordiske Komité för Bygningsbestemmelser), representing all the Scandinavian countries, considers noise control as one of its basic responsibilities. The limitation on traffic noise in Sweden is set to guarantee that "less than 20 percent of the population will be annoyed," according to Dr.

Schultz. This compares with 25 percent in the more lenient Netherlands and in France.

Paris was once known as the city where motorists, however excited, did not blow their horns. This self-control vanished in the tensions of the last few years. "Monsieur Silence" hopes to force a return to the great days of the past by raising the maximum fine from the present $12 to $120. Monsieur Silence, the nickname by which the noise-control official is known, belongs to an environmental ministry formed in early 1971. An Anti-Noise League, subsidized by the government, has been active for some years.

The Swiss, in an imaginative approach to law enforcement, organized a Police Anti-Noise Brigade in Lausanne in 1959. It is made up of five policemen armed with sound-level meters. They do most of their detective work at night. The Zurich Polytechnic offers policemen courses on acoustics and noise-control practices. In the Vaud municipalities in 1969 a moped (motorbike) campaign was launched and 8,520 were examined. A few moped owners hid their bicycles, but most cooperated. The Swiss Touring Club puts notices in its bulletins to remind members about legislation, and the Automobile Club is active in sound-abatement efforts.

When a policeman in Bermuda stops a motorbike or car for noise, he orders the driver to bring the vehicle to a test station. The muffler is removed and cut in half on the spot. Inspectors have often discovered that the contents had been taken out so that hot rod or motorcycle could make more noise. The muffler was welded back together so skillfully that no one could tell from the outside what had been done to it on the inside. Those whose muffler deceit is unmasked lose driving privileges for a time.

The difficulty of testing all cars and trucks in cities larger than those of Bermuda has often held back enforcement of noise laws. "Inspection certification in New York, for example, has been left to garages," said Columbia University's Cyril Harris. "Each garage is in a different area with a different background noise level, so inspections are not standardized. And the inspection brings an economic benefit that the owner does not want to give up no matter how noisy his location."

It also is hard to identify noise violators on the road.

"On many nights I stood out on the Thruway watching troopers measure the noise being made by trucks. A noisy truck would approach, and then as it passed the microphone, the driver would lift his foot off the accelerator, and the sound level would drop," said Christine K. Helwig, Supervisor of Mamaroneck, New York.

Tire screech, particularly from trucks, is even more annoying to people living near highways than engine noise and is harder to deal with. The sound becomes most intense at speeds of more than 50 miles per hour. Tread type affects sound production, and the rib tire is typically nine decibels quieter than the crossbar and 23 decibels softer than the suction-cup recap. As most automobiles have rib tires only, trucks are the chief source of tire noise. The sound produced by a tractor-trailer combination with 18 tires—including some new rib, some half-worn crossbars, and some new retreads—was tested at 35 miles per hour; the tire noise was found to be greater than that of the engine.

It is commonly believed that a retread tire is worse than all the rest. Some are noisier, but others are not, National Bureau of Standards tests have shown.

Another frequently repeated statement that needs reexamination, according to the bureau, is that the older the tire, the more noise it makes. This is true, but only up to a point. When half-worn, tires are indeed noisier than when they are new, but after that, some get quieter and others noisier. It would be helpful if tire manufacturers were to time-test each tire type for noise and describe its probable future to the buyer. The aging process, says one theory, is related to the gradual development of pockets in the tire. These retain air, and when the tire turns the air is squeezed out, making a characteristic sound. But in some types of tires the pockets tend to disappear with wear. Tires with a crossbar tread were the most affected by age in a study conducted by General Motors Corporation and five truck tire manufacturers.

In general, the heavier the load, the louder the screech. Observers near a highway noted that an approaching truck was rather quiet for its size. It turned off the road to pick up a cargo. When the truck returned, fully loaded, the level of tire noise had gone up by two to four decibels. This truck was using rib tires. Had it been equipped with crossbar or suction-cup recap tires, sound would have increased by seven to nine decibels when it carried freight.

Only the old can remember a time when a huge railroad network carried the nation's freight, a car was the plaything of the rich or enterprising, and highway noise was not much of a worry. As the number of trucks and cars has mounted, the set of decibel levels produced by each has multiplied to reach staggering proportions. People living near highways can close themselves off from the outside world in a house with thick walls, double windows and doors, and air conditioning. It is an effective way of escaping noise, but many refuse to hide like this. A pleasanter approach to noise protection has been suggested: the use of trees, shrubs, and grass as sound absorbers. Where hard pavements or roads reflect sound, plants and soft ground take some of it in.

Dense tropical jungle reduces noise by about six to seven decibels per 100 feet. American stands of trees do as well.

"Reductions of sound levels in the order of five to eight decibels are common and attenuations of 10 decibels . . . are not unusual for wide belts of tall dense trees," was the finding of a study in southeastern Nebraska by Drs. David I. Cook and David F. Van Haverbeke, for the Department of Agriculture and the University of Nebraska College of Agriculture.

Others have noted that a two-foot-thick cypress hedge cuts down high-frequency noise by roughly four decibels.

A single row of dense shrubs backed by a row of taller trees together formed a 20-foot barrier that successfully screened homes from car noise, Drs. Cook and Van Haverbeke reported. When heavy trucks made up a large part of the traffic, then particularly wide belts of trees were needed.

A family, much troubled by the highway noise battering their ground-floor apartment, moved two stories higher. Traffic sounds, particularly of truck tires, are just as loud 50 feet up as on the ground, so they were no better off. If trees are to bring any relief to people like these tenants, they must be extremely tall and leafy.

Many of those who moved to the country seeking peace and quiet were frustrated in their aim when highways were cut through nearby property. Trees were felled and ground cleared for miles around. This is particularly unfortunate, because speed limits in rural areas tend to be high, resulting in increased sound levels. At least there is room for correcting the mistake and bringing back trees and shrubs. To keep the noise of fast-moving highway traffic from disturbing nearby farmers and owners of country homes, groves of trees must be 65 to 100 feet wide, depending on how heavy the travel. Those trees in the center rows should be 45 or more feet tall, and the edge of the stand be no more than 50 to 80 feet away from the road. Belts of trees in suburban areas where traffic limits are lower need be only 20 to 50 feet wide, preferably surrounded with a line of six- to eight-foot-tall shrubs.

Appealing though the idea of planting is, many noise experts consider it not worth the trouble and cost. They maintain that the number of trees and shrubs needed to do any good is excessive.

About 150 trees would be required to produce any meaningful noise attenuation for a relatively small piece of ground, pointed out George E. Winzer, who heads the urban noise-abatement research program for the Department of Housing and Urban Development.

Were it possible to select the perfect sound-absorbing plants, the concept might become more feasible, and a number of botanists are working along this line. They are determining which types are best at taking in soundwaves of one or another frequency. Subtle differences in capacity emerged from a study of dense and thin foliage and soft ground carried out by Dr. Donald E. Aylor of the Connecticut Agricultural Experiment Station. A dense corn crop was planted; any other crop with heavy leaves could be expected to react in the same way. Dr. Aylor found that the low-frequency noise could get through the corn, but a considerable quantity of soundwaves of higher frequency was absorbed. Hemlock and pine trees, which have scanty foliage, and bare brush have usually been considered useless as sound absorbers. But this did not prove to be altogether the case. While less effective than the corn, they were by no means worthless. Low-frequency soundwaves, again, were able to slip past, but the bare trees were fairly effective in stopping the high. A rather different pattern was observed with soft ground. When the frequency was moderately low, the sound was absorbed. Soil did not take in soundwaves at the very low or very high ends of the frequency range.

Such newly gained knowledge could be put to practical use around the highway, Dr. Aylor explained. Noise often reaches a peak near the toll booths where trucks start up with a roar. As this roar is fairly low in frequency, it could in part be absorbed by a narrow band of soft ground set around the toll booths. Cars traveling at high speed, on the other hand, produce higher-frequency noise. Stands of leafy trees and lines of shrubs alongside the highway might take in the worst of this. This would be a drastic change from the time-honored, but unhappy custom of leveling trees alongside the roads.

An immensity of sound **141**

This has had the doubly unfortunate result of destroying beauty that could have rested the eyes of the drivers and also of allowing noise to travel far beyond a highway's boundaries.

Even those who view plantings as an inefficient way of muffling noise agree they are the most effective at reducing its annoyance. Plants achieve this in part by screening out actual noise, and in part by their very presence.

Residents of an apartment building near a highway complained bitterly and often about the noise, goes one often-told story. The sound was measured. Then a single row of trees was planted, blocking off the view of the road. Although a second series of sound measurements showed the few trees to have produced absolutely no reduction, not a single complaint was made thereafter.

All senses are involved in the reaction to the outside world. The beauty of the poplar, elm, willow, juniper, and arborvitae compensate in some measure for the ugliness of noise and noise-makers. A curtain of green stands between the onlooker and the scene of heavily loaded trucks and cars whizzing by.

In areas where plants cannot flourish, berms, the barriers of earth, rock, plastic, or concrete, can be used to attenuate highway noise. In Baltimore a road was to be tunneled under a park where families went to picnic and play ball. The earth and rock from the tunnel were collected and used to make sound-absorbing barriers, and Baltimore residents continued to enjoy the long summer afternoons in the park.

Another highway in Baltimore was cut through an area where there was a large outdoor theater. "To be or not to be" is often drowned out under such circumstances by tire and engine roar. This time a 15-foot-high acoustic barrier was put up; it was made of a transparent acrylic plastic that let the light through and did not look bulky. The level of traffic noise in bedrooms of houses nearby was 19 decibels lower than it had been before the berm was erected. The theater audiences found the voices of the actors more audible than the sound from the cars. Drama had triumphed over noise.

AND FROM THE AIR 14

A HOME-OWNER *was forced to move out of his once-pleasant home because of almost continuous jet plane flights at low altitudes. The house and land were sold to a church. And when the planes fly over during the Sunday morning service, "we simply stop," says the minister, "and offer a little silent prayer for the pilot."*

Not all Americans feel quite so charitable, and many consider themselves in need of action as well as prayer. In one community 800 people drove their cars to a nearby airport, then got out and marched around the Federal Aviation Administration building as a protest. Civic groups representing 11,000 citizens in the New York area joined to threaten demonstrations blocking traffic to and from airports every summer weekend.

The city of Inglewood, California, with an extensive noise-monitoring program compared the average flyover noise of planes, airline by airline. A five-decibel difference was measured. When this information was published, the noisier airlines began to change some of their flight procedures.

Communities periodically try to take matters into their own hands and prevent aircraft harassment. While a number of local laws have been enforced, some of the most significant have been struck down by higher courts. A committee in Hempstead, New York, clocked flights and learned that every minute an airplane flew over the spire of Saint Boniface Church in nearby Elmont. The local government passed a ruling placing specific limits on the amount of noise that would be tolerated over the town both by day and at night. A countersuit was promptly filed and a federal judge ruled that the Hempstead ordinance could not be enforced.

A key case was lost in 1953 when All American Airways, Inc., brought suit against a Cedarhurst, New York, ordinance banning flights over the village at altitudes of less than 1,000 feet. The basis of the judgment was that the "Federal Government has pre-empted the regulation of such flights in the interest of safety."

The preemption principle was upheld by the United States Supreme Court in May, 1973. It sustained a lower court decision that the city of Burbank, California, lacked the constitutional right to ban night flights.

This ruling could mean that other city and state regulations will be thrown out by the courts. Yet some could slip through a loophole in the Supreme Court decision: No ruling was made about the legality of regulations put into effect by proprietors of airports. Many of the most stringent rulings have been passed by local governors.

Subjected to enormous pressure on all sides—"we're in a no-man's-land between the airlines and the people," Tom Callaghan, assistant to the executive director of the Massachusetts Port Authority, has said—airport operators are the ones held liable in damage suits. This principle was set by the Griggs case brought in 1962 against Allegheny County, Pennsylvania, operator of the Greater Pittsburgh Airport. Griggs was a property-owner's suit charging damage produced by planes flying over the house. The county lost and the precedent was set.

It is hardly surprising then that the Port Authority of New York and New Jersey has set a limit of 112 PNdB (Perceived Noise in Decibels) for takeoffs over residential areas and has limited planes to certain runways at night. The Los Angeles International Airport governors have a set of extremely rigorous orders limiting night flights and forbidding operations at any time by noisy planes. The airport must be approached at night from the ocean side, rather than land.

But California citizens are not content to leave it at that. At the present time about $5 billion in damage claims is pending (settlement, to be sure, is usually a fraction of the claim), based on a recent court decision demanding even more of the airport operator than did Griggs. In Nestle against the City of Santa Monica for the first time harm to a person as well as to property was accepted as grounds for damages. The initial reaction in Los Angeles was that it might be necessary to close the airport, which would never be able to afford the judgments. The airport is still open, to be sure, and expected to remain so.

Those airport authorities that have been lax, despite Nestle and Griggs, in curbing noise might be forced into greater vigor by federal statute, as is favored by the Environmental Protection Agency. Before the Noise Control Act of 1972 was passed, environmentalists had lobbied for the bill to place all final rulings on aircraft and airport noise as well as enforcing powers in the hands of this agency. As passed, the Federal Aviation Administration retains a good deal of power in making decisions; whenever safety is a consideration, it can act alone. Still, the environmental agency has a number of weapons at its disposal, such as the right to comment and object, if necessary, to the environmental impact statement that must be submitted before any new airport or aircraft can gain approval. In addition, task force groups have grappled with the problem and come out in favor of federal regulation of aircraft and airport noise. Legislation should be designed, they say, to bring down the cumulative noise level calculated on the basis of all airport operations around the clock. The greatest amount of attention would be paid to ways of cutting the amount of noise reaching the people who live nearby. This could mean not only restrictions on noisy aircraft, but also changes in timetables to prevent an endless series of landings and takeoffs during the hours when they are most troublesome.

Each airport proprietor is to draw up a list of ways that noise could be reduced at his airport. The Federal Aviation Administration can force operators to make and carry out such a plan by refusing to grant airport certification if they do not. The government agency is now a financial supporter of airports, granting funds. The current grant agreement with the Los Angeles airport contains a clause ordering operations to be kept within acceptable noise limits.

Congress, say Environmental Protection Agency spokesmen, should be "unusually intense" in seeing how the Federal Aviation Administration carries out these regulations. Should it be too casual, the environmental agency would like to take over the job.

Ultimately, it is intended, land around airports will be limited to industry. The Environmental Protection Agency is establishing a new division to deal with land use. But until now it has seemed easier to control the noise of airport operations than to move the people away. The shortage of housing in the past few decades coupled with the growth of airports has brought jet planes distressingly close to the living room. In Canada, for example, airports were built in areas that were then isolated. Today those areas have become parts of Montreal and Toronto, and apartment buildings stand within a few hundred feet of the runways. Everyone agrees that creating a buffer zone between airport and residential area, and putting light industry there, is a sound plan. Making it happen, however, is another matter, considering the expense of buying houses, the resistance by home-owners to relocation, and the difficulty of finding industries willing and able to move. Then, too, those living in communities near airports, even though harassed by noise, do not extend welcoming hands to industry. One large company applied for a zoning law change to allow use of a site close to a suburban airport. This was greeted by outraged local opinion: The coming of a sizable industrial concern would change the charming character of the town. Permission was refused.

Careless airport planning has made the situation as bad as possible. A study by Sweden's Stockholm County Council showed that disturbing aircraft noise would have been reduced or eliminated for 11,000 people had the runways been built in another direction. Sweden is a small country. Airport planning has been equally heedless elsewhere; only the number of people involved is greater.

While California, which learned a hard lesson from the ruinous Los Angeles home purchase plan, has passed a zoning law and given each county an Airport Land Use Commission, it will take a long time for benefits to be felt.

In the meantime, those suffering from aircraft noise must depend on changes not only in the design, but also in the way planes are operated. The noisiest of the older planes can be piloted so that less sound reaches the ground than comes from a more modern plane flown without regard to those living below. While a plane needs full power for takeoff, the pilot can cut back the engines while climbing over areas with homes, and then return to full power to complete its climb. Anyone whose home in an airport community is beyond the three-mile mark will be benefited by a Federal Aviation Administration proposal for a mandatory two-segment approach and landing procedure. Sound reaching people in housing developments uncomfortably close to airports would be reduced by five to 15 decibels, said the administrator of the aviation agency. The plane would begin its descent when about eight miles away from the landing runway but while still at a high altitude. It would start down at a sharper angle than has been customary in the past. The aircraft would glide on a five- to six-degree slope until it got to within about three miles of the target. At this point the pilot would shift and take the plane in at the standard three-degree-angled slope for landing. Cost of the necessary instrumentation would be about $35,000 per plane.

Some of the factors influencing aircraft noise production are beyond the control of man. Wind, weather, and temperature all play a part in determining how far the sound will travel. The maneuverability of the plane can also be limited.

"Aircraft sound is louder in cold air," Columbia University's noise expert, Dr. Paul Borsky, has commented. "But when the air is hot the plane cannot climb as fast, so this cancels out the advantage."

However ideal the flying conditions and however modern the airplane, that amount of noise reduction which might be considered acceptable by day is utterly objectionable at night. The Port Authority of New York and New Jersey has reported 123 flights at Kennedy International Airport during a typical July night, 41 at Newark, and nine at LaGuardia. In addition, about one-third of the nation's mail and half the freight is moved at night.

Anything less than a complete shutdown of nighttime operations does not seem to help. Maintenance work at night has been prohibited at Boston's Logan Airport, and yet "complaints keep pouring in," said Mr. Callaghan. Although the Federal Aviation Administration has been maintaining that "the curfew is not an attractive solution" because of the difficulty of scheduling and offering adequate service, government attitudes are changing. The National Airport at Washington, D.C., run by the government, has a curfew.

And paradoxically, the Burbank case in which the curfew was defeated may win the day for the curfew, after all. "A very extraordinary occurrence" took place while the right of Burbank to forbid nighttime operations was being argued before the Supreme Court, reported Nicholas C. Yost, Deputy Attorney General of California: "The United States switched sides."

The Department of Transportation asked the Department of Justice to file a brief declaring "there simply is no general federal policy in favor of night flights by aircraft over densely populated residential districts." Insiders noted that many interested parties read the brief before its presentation to the court; despite considerable pressure, the department refused to abandon its new stance.

Perhaps airports in the United States will be allowed to follow the example set by many abroad. At least 25 airports in Europe and some in Asia do ban night flights. In a number, as at Japan's Osaka airport the regulation is strictly enforced. But in many others, the ban is loosely defined.

No takeoffs or landings at night are allowed at France's Orly and Le Bourget airports. The only exceptions allowed are emergency and postal planes.

"A friend counted 6,000 emergency and postal night flights at Orly in 1969," remarked Dr. Schultz of Bolt Berenek and Newman. "There were about 3,000 at Le Bourget."

Whatever the schedule, the one plane that is invariably viewed with distrust is the newest, the supersonic transport. Of all aircraft nuisance, none has aroused greater opposition or produced greater concern than one that has so far been experienced by relatively few: the sonic boom.

"I wrote out a charter for an organization and nine people joined," said Dr. William A. Shurcliff, Harvard physicist who started the Citizens League Against the Sonic Boom in 1967. "By mid-1970, it had 5,000 members."

The sonic boom is a unique and unwanted by-product of rapid travel. When a plane flies faster than the speed of sound, 660 miles per hour at 35,000 feet, the air is compressed into shock waves behind and beneath the craft. As these hit the earth a loud explosive bang is heard that is comparable to a nearby explosion or a thunderclap. These shock waves can be heard and felt by anyone living within a median 50-mile radius beneath the flight path. The intensity of the boom is most often between two and four pounds per square foot.

A recent discovery, the "superboom," produces pressures three to six times greater than those of the regular one. The superboom is the result of a combination of factors that luckily occur seldom, involving particular atmospheric conditions, temperature, wind velocity, shape of the plane, its speed, and altitude. The customary boom is more than enough to annoy, say those on the ground.

"The citizens of Oklahoma City never did accept or become accustomed to the boom," said Professor Lipscomb of the University of Tennessee.

He was commenting on tests in Oklahoma City in 1964 when as many as eight booms a day were produced by supersonic flights. There were 15,452 complaints and 4,901 damage claims, of which 289 were paid. Most suits here and abroad charged injury to walls, ceilings, and windows. One home-owner in Europe sued for the equivalent in his currency of 67 cents to pay for the glue he had to buy to stick back two tiles that had fallen from his kitchen ceiling. He won his case.

Whatever the damages, as the environmental agency's noise abatement chief Meyer has said: "Indemnification does not take away the injury."

Nature itself appears outraged when the ground is shaken by the boom. One day in late summer a Navajo Indian was walking on the reservation near the Canyon de Chelly in Arizona. All at once he heard a bang and saw a big piece of an overhanging cliff fall off when the shock wave hit. A succession of booms followed, and each time some more of the rock face was shaken loose. The falling rocks damaged or destroyed cliff dwellings that had been cut into the canyon in prehistoric times.

"What is a 3,000- or 4,000-year-old prehistoric ruin worth? It just disintegrated under the sonic boom. What is the face of a cliff in Mesa Verde worth? It is shattered off and now is at the bottom of the canyon," complained George H. Hartzog, who has served as director of the National Park Service.

Nature lovers and others who refused to accept such disintegration joined to demand that the United States cease efforts to built the supersonic plane. A coalition was formed, operating out of Sierra Club offices, with G. A. Soucie, director of Friends of the Earth, as chairman. The political action group Common Cause entered the battle, as did the Environmental Defense Fund, formed by a group of scientists and lawyers, and the Association of American Scientists. In May, 1971, Congress voted to halt the Boeing Company's development program.

With this as precedent, the Federal Aviation Administration in March, 1973, banned supersonic flights over the United States by commercial aircraft, except for research purposes in designated test areas.

"I have been writing to the Federal Aviation Administration about every three months for six years urging them to make such a ban," commented Dr. Shurcliff. "Earlier, they had scoffed at the idea."

Development of supersonic aircraft technology may continue, but an application to exceed the speed of sound, known as Mach 1, is to be rejected if "such action is necessary to protect and enhance the environment."

The supersonic transport plane presents major engine-noise problems in addition to the boom, producing 129 PNdB on the sideline.

"A major breakthrough" will be needed, said space agency experts, to bring sound down to more endurable levels.

Another great blow to a supersonic future was struck by United States airlines which early in 1973 decided to drop their options to buy the British-French Concorde. Aside from the environmental dangers, the fantastically expensive SSTs were viewed as uneconomic. This left only a handful of orders on the books. At last in 1974, the British government declared itself prepared to concede failure and began efforts to persuade the French to go along with this decision.

Many major airports threaten to forbid the supersonic planes from landing. Americans have been markedly cool to the coming of these foreign planes. Some city governments have passed legislation banning supersonic planes from their airports. Though these ordinances have thus far not been upheld by the courts, they have carried some weight, nonetheless. Countries abroad have similarly refused to extend a welcome to the planes. The first ones were hardly off the ground before legislation to ban them came up for discussion in Sweden, Switzerland, Ireland, and elsewhere. A Swiss citizens' action group rapidly collected 50,000 signatures urging a referendum on legislation keeping the supersonic planes away. Organizations such as Australia's Project to Stop the Concorde and England's Anti-Concorde Project proliferated.

The Soviets have also had some bad luck with their Tupolev-144, capable of cruising at 1,550 miles per hour. In order to make this plane more profitable, it was redesigned to carry 140 passengers instead of the 128 of the Concorde. A TU–144, however, exploded and crashed during a demonstration flight at an international air show in Paris on June 3, 1973. This disaster was seen by thousands. The following year the Soviets, in what appeared to be an effort to counteract the bad publicity announced changes in design and described an intensified test schedule. A veteran Soviet pilot declared he was flying the tests "without the slightest hesitation." The newspaper *Pravda* said the plane was being produced, but figures were not given.

According to current plans, the TU–144, or "Concordski" as some Westerners have dubbed it, will start by flying within the Soviet Union, through remote Siberia, and next to Asia.

"Perhaps in time it [the Trans-Siberian Railroad] will be superseded by the supersonic jet," remarked the narrator of a National Geographic television special on Siberia.

Like the Soviets, the British and French are not prepared to keep their SSTs in the hangar and continue to plan transatlantic commercial service. They recognize that a ban on the boom is not the same as a ban on the supersonic plane. It can fly across the ocean at the greatest possible speed and then slow to a normal subsonic rate when approaching land. Although the Port of New York Authority refused to allow the Concorde to land following a much-publicized trip during the summer of 1974, the plane did find sanctuary in Boston.

It has been proposed that permission to use American airports be granted for a specified number of flights each week.

While pointing out that it is "not certain whether the United States will ever build the airplane," the National Aeronautics and Space Administration is working to improve the engineering of the SST, so as to keep the "option open."

And no one engages in research and development without hope that the product will ultimately come into use. The conviction that the SSTs are coming is expressed in a variety of unexpected places. In the spring of 1973, for example, a leading women's fashion magazine began an article on travel paraphernalia with the matter-of-fact comment that when the supersonic planes come into use, weight will be an even more important factor than it is now.

The federal regulation forbidding the boom does not cover military aircraft, and these are the source of the booms experienced by most Americans. The damage in the Canyon de Chelly and Mesa Verde was produced by flights of military planes. The Air Force in the summer of 1972 displayed its F–15 fighter which can reach a speed of Mach 2.5. The *New York Times* reporter present at the unveiling reported that with "engines keening like a banshee," it taxied onto the ramp. This plane, and its wail, will not be unique; there is word that the Air Force wants whole fleets of small fighters capable of going at twice the speed of sound. Reconnaissance jets can do better than that. Traveling three times as fast as sound, a spy plane crossed the Atlantic in 1974 in just over one hour and 55 minutes.

Preventing the sonic boom by keeping the plane's speed below that of sound eliminates the time-saving advantage. Some other solutions are being suggested.

"At a speed just slightly greater than that of sound, up to Mach 1.15, and at a cruising altitude of about 60,000 feet, the boom would not be apparent on the ground," the Federal Aviation Administration's environmental scientist has said.

An opposite concept of using greater rather than lesser speeds, although somewhat more difficult to achieve, is also being urged. Hypersonic planes, going at speeds six or more times that of sound, produce lesser booms, but over a larger area.

A more perfect solution to the boom problem may eventually be found through advances in engineering and design that lift the SST above its present limits.

"If the plane can go high enough, the boom will not reach the ground," said Dr. Henning E. von Gierke of the Aerospace Medical Research Laboratories. "That is the goal of NASA research—to fly above 10,000 feet."

Achieving that goal will take many years and military and foreign planes are in the air right now. Opponents abroad tell that a few years ago the Concorde flew over an old farmhouse in the village of Mauron, France, just as a farmer, his wife, and eight farmworkers were sitting down to lunch. "Le bang," as the boom is known in France, was heard, and the building shook. The roof beams collapsed, letting fall the eight tons of barley that had been stored in the attic, and burying the farmers. The neighbors rushed to dig the people out of the barley, but by then three were dead and one badly hurt.

The Americans have no monopoly on damage suits. The British government's Department of Trade and Industry in 1972 reported actual compensation of £15,587 for "structural" damage, £19,669 for harm to animals, and £366 for a variety of other injuries, with 27 more claims outstanding.

Damage to property is often hard to prove definitively, nonetheless. The National Trust in England reported that the boom caused by a flight of the Concorde injured sixteenth-century glass at a manor house in Cornwall. On the other hand, no harm was done to the four ancient cathedrals selected by the Church of England for study by the Royal Aircraft Establishment. While conceding that there is no firm scientific proof that the SST was to blame, the chief government architect for the Alsace-Lorraine area of France viewed it as a likely cause of the "dramatic acceleration in damage to the stonework" of the Strasbourg Cathedral. Stones have split, flaked, or burst. The cathedral was begun in the eleventh century, and the spire was completed in 1439.

One of the most annoyed of all home-, or castle-, owners, lives in the village of St. Julien de Lampon, France. He is the proud possessor of the eleventh-century castle of Fenelon. The walls are seven feet thick, but over the centuries the mortar between the huge stone blocks has dried out. One day in spring the Concorde flew overhead. "Le bang" caused the west tower to crumble.

THE "WHISPER" PLANES

"W H E N *supersonic flying became a reality, the phenomenon of the sonic boom had not been predicted.*"

These startling words were written long after the fact by a National Aeronautics and Space Administration expert for the *Journal of the Acoustical Society of America.*

It had, of course, been known that a shock wave will follow when an object is propelled through air at speeds greater than that of sound. No one had realized that this wave produced by a high-altitude plane would have such far-flung effects, hitting the ground with violence and noise.

The booms were a popular feature of air shows in the first few years following Air Force Captain Charles Yeager's supersonic flight of 1947. It took ten years and experimental cross-country flights to awaken people to the recognition that the boom was not an exciting act, but a disturbance.

The failure to predict what a supersonic plane would do is understandable in that there were no actual precedents. But the fact that airplanes would be noisy has been apparent from the moment man took to the skies. Aircraft development has been characterized by a refusal to look to the obvious noise that would be generated by fleets of planes and to plan ways of reducing it.

In the beginning noise must have seemed a trivial price to pay for the miracle of flight. Since the mythical Icarus fell into the sea when the wax of his wings melted in the sun's rays, man has sought to imitate the birds. At last it had happened. The initial flights may have seemed as exciting to people living at that time as spacecraft voyages to the moon do to us today. The sound of the rocket that propels the capsule upwards reaches levels that would never be tolerated under any other circumstances. The noise both now and then may have added to the excitement and made people more aware of the wonder.

Residents of old San Juan in Puerto Rico in 1974 went to court to complain that handclapping, loud praying, and singing from the Pentecostal Church of God was troubling them. The church was fined, and the decision was appealed. Pentecostal church officials not only reject soundproofing and closed doors, but actually employ sound systems that will send the noise out onto the street. The belief is that new worshippers are attracted by the sounds of prayers and singing and that these should be audible throughout crowded residential neighborhoods.

It might seem that airlines and those in charge of airports are similarly seeking converts to air travel by forcing people living close by to hear the sound of planes coming in to land or taking off. And like the residents of San Juan, those close to airports are balking at the noise made by aircraft.

One home-owner in an airport community on Long Island is said to have rigged up a huge medieval catapult in his backyard. He used it to hurl muffins, prepared for the purpose by his wife, at the low-flying airplanes.

When jet aircraft first were flown, the greatest noise from the turbojet engines was caused by the exhaust mixing at great speed with the surrounding air. This occurred at takeoff when the plane was being thrust upward. Then the turbofan engine came into use. This was quieter, because it pulled in more air and expelled this at lower jet speed. But to the original sound annoyance, attenuated but by no means solved, was added a new one—the whine of the fan. For a long time, though, flying was reserved for the wealthy, for the businessman, the statesman. The minute-by-minute takeoff or landing was still a nightmare for the future.

That nightmare had become reality when in 1969, 63 years after the Wright brothers made their first flights, the Federal Aviation Administration at last passed an amendment, the 36th, to the Federal Aviation Regulation.

"Part 36 is the first government ruling requiring aircraft manufacturers to consider noise as a design parameter," said the Federal Aviation Administration's chief environmental scientist.

Part 36 demands that new planes achieve levels at takeoff that range from 93 to a maximum of 108 EPNdB (Effective Perceived Noise in Decibels), depending on weight of plane, and from 102 to 108 for approach and sideline.

"New jet planes would have been louder by 10 to 15 decibels if we had not had that ruling," declared the Federal Aviation Administration, citing the sound level produced by the McDonnell Douglas DC–10, the first plane to meet the new noise emission standards. This is about 15 decibels quieter than the long-range DC–8 and from 4 to 10 decibels lower than the Boeing 727. The Boeing 747, designed just before the perfection of additional sound-control techniques, was allowed some exceptions to the standards. Even so, its noise levels are no greater on takeoff and are less on approach and on the sideline than those made by other four-engine transports, half its size. The cost for acoustic treatment of 16 747 aircraft at American Airlines was roughly $4 million, said company vice-president Kolk, and the weight of the acoustical material in each plane was equivalent to that of 26 passengers.

While there can be no doubt that planes have been quieted to some extent, they have far to go to achieve the effects claimed for them. Indeed, at present, the word "whisper" used in much airplane advertising has taken on an Orwellian connotation. In homes near airports where the "whisper" planes land and take off, residents converse in shouts.

A goal of a 10-decibel-per-decade noise reduction has been expressed by government transportation officials. Contracts have been given to the General Electric Company and Boeing Company to design a "Quiet Engine." The models that have been made and tested give only 90 EPNdB at takeoff, compared to 104 for the newest airplanes to receive Federal Aviation Administration certification.

Yet those attending a National Aeronautics and Space Administration Conference in 1972 were told: "The Quiet Engine as it exists today cannot be used on airliners; it is an experimental engine."

The reason, as acoustical engineer Goodfriend had predicted: "This engine is much too heavy for airline use."

Though the entire "Quiet Engine" is not yet feasible, many of its features could be applied to current plane design. Aircraft companies have been content to meet government standards, an improvement over the past, to be sure, but by no means the degree of silence possible today. Word is out that engineers are developing a commercial engine that is capable of achieving noise levels well below those of the regulation. Although it could fly a plane, manufacturers need not put it into general production. If instead they choose less advanced models, the next generation of planes would be unnecessarily noisy, though somewhat quieter than its predecessors.

But even were new aircraft to achieve the best of all possible goals, the question of what to do with the huge fleets of older Boeing 737s, 727s, 707s, and Douglas DC–8s and DC–9s has haunted those who would control aircraft noise. The 15 major airlines still have 1,820 turbofan craft. These could be brought to Part 36 requirements only by major changes.

After five years of study and the urging of the environmental agency, the Federal Aviation Administration proposed that a rule be passed requiring that old planes either be redesigned or put out of the airways by a target date of July, 1978. Changes in engineering, or retrofit, would have to be extensive enough to make old planes sound like new ones. All must be brought to the point of meeting the standards of Part 36. It would probably be uneconomic to redesign the old turbojet airplanes, and these are gradually being retired from service.

"This retrofit proposal represents the biggest program we have ever had in the field of noise control," said an aviation agency spokesman.

The proposal rapidly ran into opposition. The aircraft industry objected to retrofit on the basis of cost, and indeed the Environmental Protection Agency has estimated that it would take $600 million and several years to follow the simplest redesign plan. The foreign airlines were even more vehement about the requirement that they alter their older aircraft in order to be allowed the use of United States airports.

The easiest, quickest, and least costly way of modifying the older planes, the environmental agency's Report to Congress on Aircraft/Airport Noise points out, is to surround the nacelle, the part of the plane housing the engine, with sound-absorbing materials. Ready-to-use kits have been designed. Modification of the engine fan itself would reduce noise further, but needs flight testing and would, in any event, cost more.

With the help of a $7 million contract from the Federal Aviation Administration, the Boeing Company has created a model for retrofit. After the nacelle is lined with sound-absorbing material, layers of thin, honeycombed metal or glass fiber are placed at or around the fan. A contest between two 707s, one retrofitted, was carried out in May, 1973. The planes flew over the countryside south of Washington, D.C., while members of government and industry and private individuals listened below and sound instruments measured levels electronically. Reductions of 15 decibels at landing and of up to 10 decibels during the climb after takeoff were recorded. The greatest improvement was in the lessening of the piercing high-frequency whine. The plane is still noisy, observers hastened to remark, but it is much better than before.

True sound relief will come only when planes are quieted, the land around airports purchased and given over to industry, all nearby housing soundproofed, and flight schedules and operating procedures revised. Cost of programs to achieve a day-night average noise level of 70 decibels by 1980 for those near airports would be $13.3 billion, and dropping to 60 decibels of sound would require $22.3 billion, the agency study pointed out.

Who would pay for the changes? A passenger "head" tax and a freight tax might be levied, a "dollars for decibels" landing fee charged, and grants and investment capital obtained from government and private sources. Should the French example be followed, the consumer will be called on to hand over his mite. A noise tax was added to plane tickets in France with so little publicity that an Englishman flying roundtrip to Paris decided that the extra 30 pence demanded of him by his travel agent was extortion. He decided to go to the airline office himself. Only then did he learn what the small sum is for. A part of the money raised is to be used to support soundproofing grants for home-owners near Orly and Le Bourget airports. United States experts have calculated that a ticket price rise to pay for retrofit of jet planes here would amount to one percent or less.

Part 36 left a number of noise loopholes, aside from retrofit, which are gradually being filled in. The Federal Aviation Administration is proposing that noise limits be set for light planes, ignored in the original rule. Even the planes used in acrobatic demonstrations in air shows would no longer be allowed to excite the viewers with excessive noise. For safety reasons, however, crop-dusting and other agricultural and fire-fighting planes would be exempted from the proposed noise standards for propeller-driven small airplanes. All the available engine power is needed for the extremely large loads carried by these planes, said the federal agency, leaving nothing over for sound-muffling devices. Where life itself is at stake, loss of hearing is a small price to pay. Many who elect to use such planes, though, are quite unaware of choosing auditory danger. Whenever hearing tests have been given to those riding in or piloting these planes regularly, a disproportionately large number is found to be deafened.

The Federal Aviation Administration is planning to develop noise regulations for the light planes, the V/STOL craft, but concedes the problems are great. The public at large does not even know what the letters stand for—Vertical/Short Take-Off and Landing. The words reveal just where the danger lies. As these planes do not need long runways, STOLports can be placed right in the midst of a busy community to add just one more noise insult. The federal agency has commented that these planes are thrust upwards by large rotors, making them noisier than conventional aircraft. The reverse thrust at landing is just as bad. Sharply angled approaches and takeoffs would help, but even when up, these short haul planes do not go as high as the jets. The sound is heard in the living rooms of the apartment houses all along the route.

When a STOLport is announced for a specific area, those who understand what this means rapidly get the word around to others in the community. Citizens' groups are vehement in their opposition to the coming of STOLports. One community board which sought to forestall the creation of a port in the Hudson River was given the opportunity to listen to an airplane passing overhead, and simulating landings and takeoffs. Although a Federal Aviation Administration official present remarked that the sound had blended in with the "ambient noise" in the street, a *New York Times* reporter on the scene pointed out that ambient noise on the street included a jack-hammer and passing buses. Recreational facilities, including a marina and a hotel at the STOLport, were being held out as lures to reduce the outcry against the short-range planes.

The National Aeronautics and Space Administration is pushing a search for the "questol," or quiet STOL. Like "whisper," this will clearly be a relative, not an absolute term.

Some Americans wistfully seek a return to an earlier type of fast-rising aircraft, the balloon. On an April weekend in 1974, a convention of balloonists gathered in the village of Farmington, Connecticut. The joy, said one, lies in the "noiseless freedom" of balloon flight. "It's the ability to float like a bird over mountains and valleys." The catch, unfortunately, is that the balloon cannot be steered, but must be carried by the wind . . . and could not substitute for the far from noiseless STOLplane.

The most widely-flown planes of the V/STOL class today are helicopters which produce noise of low frequency that can be heard for greater distances than higher-pitched sounds. At a distance of 500 feet, the light helicopter gives forth from 78 to 86 dBA, depending on engine type, while the medium-weight plane produces 88 to 96 dBA. A feeling of despair about a solution to helicopter noise is common. And, to a certain extent, it is valid. To date, even military helicopters have not been quieted sufficiently to conceal their approach from an enemy.

Nonetheless, helicopter noise could be cut down by the use of several techniques: the number of revolutions per second made by the engine can be reduced, the shape of the blades altered, and ways of muffling the engine exhaust improved. If such technology were applied, the sound levels could be brought down by 10 to 20 decibels, with the greatest reductions attained by the lightest helicopters. Realists comment that such improvements are not likely to be seen in this decade.

In the meantime, helicopters are used not only by businessmen saving themselves travel time and inconvenience, but also by the police for medical emergencies, searches, rescues, and traffic surveys. Police heliports are often of necessity in the midst of populated areas.

While the public will accept a police heliport, opposition to industrial installations is inexorable.

"We want to do the right thing," the spokesman for a large corporation responded to the Committee to Save Our Serenity. Citizens of a charming Connecticut community had formed the committee in an attempt to head off the coming of the company helicopter pad.

"Doing the right thing" never seems to mean abandoning the project, and short of that, can any company approach this noble goal with the helicopters available to it today?

THE PEOPLE AGAINST 16
NOISE

"MY LIVING *belongs to that speaker," said the owner of a record store ordered to reduce the volume of the loudspeaker that blared music out onto the street.*

"To you it's a living, but to other people it's a nuisance," replied the noise inspector.

The sound in another record shop was found equivalent to that heard on a subway platform in rush hour.

"Whether it hurts your business, all I do is enforce the law," said the inspector, referring to New York City's noise code.

The problem of reconciling a pleasant environment with the right to do business remains essentially unchanged since those seventeenth-century days when British authorities threatened to pull down the tannery with its noxious odors.

Many citizens today are driven to the point of demanding that businesses improve or be pulled down.

"We'll only be happy when you're closed," a neighbor told the owner of a side street cabaret which opened at 10 P.M. and stayed open to 4 A.M. three nights a week, attracting large, noisy crowds.

What could be done? residents asked the police. They were urged to form a block association and raise money to hire a lawyer to present their grievances in court.

"In order to have legislation passed, we need a groundswell of public opinion," a Congressman explained a few years ago to people calling him to complain about noise. This groundswell eventually mounted and the federal law followed.

Taking citizens' action in New York as typical of what has been happening all over the country, the battle against Thruway noise began many years ago when residents of the community of Larchmont were awakened night after night by trucks roaring down the highway. Neighbors joined in protest. One group sought an injunction to close the Thruway altogether, a desperate measure with no hope of passage. But the complaints became so numerous that officials of nine municipalities along the route had to respond by appropriating funds for a Thruway Noise Abatement Committee.

"Of 300,000 people living in these communities, we estimate that certainly 100,000 are affected by noise," commented Christine K. Helwig, permanent chairman of the committee.

Years of effort were devoted to getting relief for these thousands. "Mrs. Helwig brought sweet womanly reason into the discussions with the truckers," said the acoustical engineer who served as consultant to the committee.

More than 300 trucks were selected at random on the New England Thruway in 1962 and 1963 and tape recordings made of their passage. One-fourth produced noise levels above 87 dBA, and 10 percent gave out 90 dBA or more. Tire noise was also investigated by a jury sitting by the side of the road at Larchmont. Trucks with high noise ratings were stopped at nearby tollbooths and their tire treads noted. Manufacturers were invited for discussion. And eventually the efforts of the committee led to passage of a pioneering state law setting decibel limits for vehicles using public highways.

Even so, quiet did not descend upon the roads around New York. "I live half a mile from the Thruway, and some nights it seems that trucks are circling the house," remarked Mrs. Helwig.

"We have spent the last five years trying to get the New York bill revised," she added. "I feel very strongly that states should put their aspirations down on paper. I think they will influence the federal government."

The ruling was not strong enough when it was passed, and it failed to make provision for the time when highways, cars, and trucks would have proliferated—although it was obvious that they must. A lack of foresight about environmental side-effects has characterized those who push for new highways.

"At the time it was built, the state had given assurance that the new six-lane superhighway would not conflict with the environment," said John French, III, president of the Quiet Highways Council, Inc., a local group, with support from the Sierra Club Foundation. It was formed in reaction to the conflict with the environment presented by the road once it was finished and in use.

"A 12-mile stretch of the highway going from Katonah to Armonk is unique in that it was built through purely residential districts," said Mr. French.

A fund of about $15,000 was raised by 70 interested citizens and the firm of Bolt Berenek and Newman was hired for a study. On a single day more than 1,000 people signed a petition asking for a hearing on demands to lower speed limits, raise muffler standards, and install barriers along a 27-mile length on the Westchester expressway. In December, 1972, a hearing was duly held by the state's departments of Environmental Conservation and Transportation, and, said Mr. French, "We provided three and a half hours of testimony."

Aircraft noise has aroused even more wrath than automotive.

The Hempstead ordinance limiting the amount of permissible airplane noise over the town is typical of local actions that failed, but that had a kind of success after all in influencing the ultimate passage of the federal bill. Behind the Hempstead ordinance was an organization supported by municipal funds, the Town-Village Noise Abatement Committee. It was run by the mayor and supervisors of the town of Hempstead and 10 neighboring villages. Estimates were that half a million people in the area were affected by aircraft noise. Many protested vociferously that they would not settle for the limits set for jet planes by the New York Port Authority.

Some years ago a few individuals in Larchmont also decided to reject aircraft noise as a fact of life. Each set out to find one other person with not only the interest, but also the spirit to complain. In this way a local organization was formed. At the same time groups of noise-harassed citizens were gathering in Yonkers and Brooklyn. Eventually all the groups got together and incorporated themselves. A council of civic organizations in New York City and the outlying counties was established with the aim of coordinating complaints and advising members on how and to whom to protest.

A great deal of stress has been placed on the right of the Environmental Protection Agency to comment on the environmental impact statement prepared by a federal agency with a new project in mind. Few people realize that the private citizen, as well as industry, and state and local agencies, has this right, too.

There is a predictable cause-and-effect response to the announcement that a new airport is to be built or an existing one enlarged.

"Our group formed as soon as it was learned that there were plans for expanding Stewart Air Force Base near Newburgh into a major jetport," declared Rod Vandivert, director of the Hudson River Valley Council, which represents conservation, civic, and business groups. "We anticipate a prolonged argument."

The council has already been to court to question New York's

The people against noise   **169**

Metropolitan Transportation Authority's intentions. Mr. Vandivert considers the "green belt" buffer zone of trees suggested by the authority as totally inadequate.

Only one new major jetport—Dallas-Forth Worth—has been built thus far in the 1970s. Yet in 1970 Congress passed a bill to encourage airport construction by offering matching grants of $280 million a year. The offer has not been taken up. The *New York Times* has attributed the blocking of planned jetports in Atlanta, Boston, Miami, Minneapolis-St. Paul, and a number of other cities directly to opposition from community and environmental groups. Even very small organizations have been successful in holding back or preventing airport construction.

Though the fuel shortage and resulting increase in airfares has, at least temporarily, cut down traffic at airports, it is inconceivable that no new jetports will ever be built or existing ones expanded. Citizens' groups remain alert.

While some organizations are formed on a temporary basis, with a specific goal, such as opposition to construction of an airport or highway; others are designed for permanence. Occasionally, an anti-pollution superagency is made up of all the conservation groups in an area. About 90 organizations have gotten under the "umbrella" of California's Planning and Conservation League. A full-time lobbyist is maintained at the state legislature to press for anti-noise legislation. He is on the scene and on guard against any plans that would increase noise, such as poorly conceived highway and airport construction and expansion.

Notable among the citywide groups has been New York's Citizens for a Quieter City, founded by Robert Alex Baron.

"I was never interested in noise until a subway was being built under my window," Mr. Baron has said. "I called the Health Department, the Police Department, and even went to Washington to the Public Health Service. No one had anything to tell me that would help. I returned home and bought earplugs and took tranquilizers. And at last I decided to found an organization to do something about noise."

Citizens for a Quieter City has taken an active role in awakening inhabitants of this noisiest of cities to the possibility that there could be quiet. In the late 1960s when everyone "knew" that construction noise must be deafening, Mr. Baron arranged to borrow a muffled air compressor and paving breaker from a company in England. These were shipped to the United States and demonstrated on the street and on television. In 1972, at the organization's urging, city officials pronounced Quiet Week. It was marked by "Operation Horn-Blower" and a "Quietude Happening" near the mall in Central Park. The 10 minutes of quiet that were to start this off had to be postponed, because the mall was given over to a rock-and-roll concert. Free hearing tests were offered all that week. Citizens for a Quieter City is now being reorganized, and Mr. Baron is considering founding or joining a national operation.

Described by founder Theodore Berland as the first national citizens anti-noise group, Citizens Against Noise, which goes under the suggestive abbreviation of C.A.N., has its headquarters in Chicago. It has declared as goals noise standards for sources ranging from home appliances to toys, trucks, cars, and aircraft; a national building code; a national public education campaign, and improvements in state and local laws.

A second organization which aims at "quieter skies and quieter lives for all" also has worked out a particularly felicitous acronyn for its name, N.O.I.S.E. from National Organization to Insure a Sound-Controlled Environment. Each year since 1972, a symposium is held, so experts and environmentalists can compare notes on current information on jet noise.

The British similarly wish quieter skies, and its Noise Abatement Society has mounted a campaign so vigorous that it was cited by the

American trade publication *Advertising Age.*

One advertisement was an open invitation to the Minister of Aviation to spend a few days with the mythical "Websters" in their retirement home. The Websters' "life should be delightful. Instead it's pure hell. . . . Because every couple of minutes . . . the house shakes. The noise is unbearable." The Minister of Aviation, on the other hand, lives far from an airport, the advertisement continues. Readers are urged to join the society before the minister "lets a great big jet hedge-hop over your front garden."

While everyone wants aircraft kept away from his door, feelings are mixed about the second major source of transportation noise, the automobile. A number of activists are as ready to ban the car as the supersonic plane. Most Americans, however, as an old vaudeville song put it, would prefer automobiles to be prohibited for "somebody else, not me." Even though, to quote former United States Supreme Court Justice Brown, "the automobile lacks one of the most attractive concomitants of pleasure-driving in the companionship of the horse," people cling doggedly to their cars. This is due to the unattractive quality of mass transit to date and, in most parts of the country, to its inconvenience. Yet the losing combination of noise, air pollution, and congestion is making people insist upon basic changes—not only in the actual design, but also in the way the car is used. What the curfew could be to aircraft, a ban on entering central parts of cities will be to cars.

The idea, startling to Americans, is neither new nor original. In Rome, Copenhagen, and Amsterdam, cars have for a number of years been prohibited from traveling on certain downtown streets. In Canada, trucks are routed away from residential streets and onto special routes.

Even in the United States the days of total automotive freedom may be numbered. A series of traffic regulations cutting down the numbers of cars in cities has been proposed by the Environmental

Protection Agency. It is aimed specifically at reducing air pollution. But where the car is involved, if air pollution goes, noise cannot be far behind.

When a New York City taxi driver heard that the Environmental Protection Agency had gone so far as to recommend "a selective ban on taxi cruising," he responded with disgust: "Conservation is all very well . . . but there's a limit!"

Any restrictions on the driving of private cars will provide badly needed havens of quiet and reduce city tensions. People will be forced onto mass transit and noise would be concentrated on streets with bus routes or held underground.

Although broader use of mass transit seems almost too obvious an approach, it is quite revolutionary. Improvements in mass transportation receive least-favored-child treatment from government agencies. In New York, as a *New York Times* editorial pointed out, buses contribute greatly to overall noise levels. Yet when funds were made available for improvement, they were spent to paint the buses blue.

This lackadaisical approach is hardly surprising. Until very recently the government agencies were not being pushed by the people. Citizens' action groups, so vigorous about aircraft and highway noise, were for years strangely indolent in pressing for quieter buses, trains, and subways.

Better maintenance of cars and tracks could reduce subway noise. Instead, the Environmental Protection Agency was told that in New York City only four miles of subway track is replaced in a year. And what of new subway lines? Acoustical experts point to comparatively low noise levels in the subways in Montreal, Mexico City, and Sapporo, Japan. Rubber wheels make much of the difference, but American mass transit officials say such tires would not fit present tracks.

A new line is to be constructed beneath Second Avenue in New York. Whatever is left undone, in terms of noise control, will be extremely hard to do later. "When we are being tied to a subway line for the next fifty years, someone should study rubber wheels. But no one is," said Columbia's Dr. Harris.

Improving mass transport and increasing its use should be only one part of an overall plan directed at protecting people from noise. Cities could be designed and highways routed in ways that keep down the sound levels reaching residential areas. Unfortunately, cities have been planned—or have grown up unplanned long ago—and basic changes are costly. New highways and secondary streets are fitted in anyhow. As a rule, road builders view it as sufficient if they depress or elevate highways over residential and hospital zones or build acoustical barriers.

Yet the use of a city plan that considers noise is not purely utopian, a dream to be espoused by wild-eyed dreamers. Cities are in a constant state of flux—expanding here, redeveloping there, adding a suburb. Even today urbanization is coming for the first time to some out-of-the-way regions. Highway construction is unending. Any change offers the opportunity for noise reduction.

A new suburb, Furuset, was recently added to the Norwegian city of Oslo. Only shops and office buildings were put up alongside the existing highway.

This type of planning is the direct result of the influence of the Nordic Committee for Building Regulations. Its blueprints could serve as models for city planning anywhere. The suggestions made by the subcommittee on noise are not mandatory. They are followed, because the citizens of the Scandinavian countries wish a quieter environment.

As an example, the peaceful sound level of 35 dBA can be attained indoors, if the noise outside is held to a 24-hour average of 59. To achieve this level, the committee in December, 1966, proposed a set of standards and rules for highway noise—Stoj og Byplan.

To show the effect the committee's plan has on urban renewal, a Dane recalled how a new highway was to be taken across a residential area and close to a hospital in Copenhagen. Instead, the city government had the road cut through a slum. Killing two birds with one stone, officials had the slum residents relocated to a quieter part of the city, and their former homes were torn down and replaced by industries.

The Scandinavian group worked out a four-zone plan to be used in cities. Factories would be placed nearest to roads, schools and business offices next, and homes in the third. In the heart of the city, the fourth zone, would be a central green or park, of the type that in past eras was a focal point for all activities. The apartment buildings ringing the green would act as a noise break. The city dweller walking through his park might think himself in the countryside as he listened to the song of the birds, the rustling of leaves.

But people grow impatient while waiting for the city they live in to be changed or for an opportunity to move to a different one that is better planned. More immediate relief could come if the ideas expressed in a convention worked out by the Scandinavian countries were generally adopted. It gives legal recognition to the obvious fact that pollution knows no boundaries. Garbage is poured into the river in one country, and flows with the water from one nation to another, fouling taste and smell for people who had nothing to do with dirtying it in the first place. Cars speed down the highways of one nation, and the winds waft the exhaust fumes over the rural areas of another.

The Frenchman who heard but could not see the strip-tease show turned to French justice for relief. But should a strip-tease show be performed in Belgium, for example, and the sound blare across the border to France, the disturbed Frenchman would have no court of appeal. The new convention would change that for citizens of Sweden, Norway, Denmark, and Finland. In terms of the environment, they would be as one. If a Swede were disturbed by the noise produced by a manufacturing plant in Norway, he could bring suit in Norway and demand a change. In the legal proceedings, he would be considered a native, not an alien. Should foxes in Finland be alarmed by the sound and vibration of a construction project in Sweden, the fox farmer could make his complaint in Sweden. The convention is designed to cover other aspects of the environment, too. If a Norwegian got an attack of asthma, because of the air pollution produced by a Norwegian factory, he might similarly ask that this be controlled or damages paid him.

The concept behind the convention could change thinking about pollution control in other countries, too. Even not-so-friendly neighbors might agree about the environment.

Any overall planning to reduce noise, whether international or domestic in scope, will come in the future, as it has in the past, only on the demand of an aroused citizenry.

In one sense, noise is not a new form of pollution. Chariots were forbidden on the streets of ancient Rome at night. Benjamin Franklin complained that the sound of carts going over the cobblestones disturbed his sleep. What is new to this menace is its scale. At no time in the past were such vast populations exposed regularly to noise. With the coming of mechanized industry, the invention of the automobile, air compressor, jet plane, electrified guitar, noise has reached the point of damaging hearing and destroying contentment.

Few silent spaces remain, almost none where a person can earn his living. Highways have been carved through land that was wilderness only recently. No boundaries exist for the aircraft passing overhead.

For a long time noise was accepted as an integral part of modern life. It has been described as the price of industrial growth, prosperity, even comfort. But a change in attitude has come. Noise no longer seems a necessary evil.

There is an awakening to the realization that industry can operate more silently, and yet be profitable, that truck tires can turn without screeching, and yet goods be carried down the nation's highways. Even the jet planes need not totally disrupt the lives of millions in order to bring passengers to their destinations.

Battery-operated buses were tested in the British city of Leeds in June, 1972. The buses are so quiet that people cannot hear them coming, and some have expressed fear of being knocked down. "What we need is something subtle, but audible," commented an official in Leeds, possibly a recording of the song of the lark, or the rustling of leaves.

Noise control lies within reach. The laws are on the books. The technology exists to quiet all noise sources. Some of the changes are simple as putting mufflers on cars. Others are as complex as coming to international agreement about jet and supersonic aircraft. But all are possible.

Only where people have refused to accept noise has quiet come. A Rhode Island law banning nighttime scheduled flights was vetoed by the government. But Providence citizens protested so vigorously that airlines rescheduled or eliminated four night flights.

There are places where drivers do not blow horns, construction crews stop work at night, where buildings are soundproofed, areas zoned for industry, and planes kept from landing and taking off during the hours when most people sleep. Few in number today, they are gradually increasing, as more individuals are insisting on quiet as necessary to their well-being and happiness.

The significance of noise pollution was recognized long ago by Robert Koch, bacteriologist, Nobel Prize-winner in 1905. He described noise as "merciless," and predicted that the day would come when man will have to fight against it as an "enemy of his health." That day has come and the fight against noise is on.

BIBLIOGRAPHY

BIBLIOGRAPHY

ACOUSTICAL MATERIALS ASSOCIATION, *The Use of Achitectural Acoustical Materials*, 1965. 2nd edition.

ACOUSTICAL SOCIETY OF AMERICA, *Abstracts*, 83rd Meeting, April 18–21, 1972.

—————, *Proceedings of the Sonic Boom Symposium*, November 3, 1965, published May, 1966.

—————, *Report on the Conference on Acoustics and Societal Problems*, Arden House, Harriman, New York, June, 1972.

AMERICAN STANDARDS ASSOCIATION, *The Relations of Hearing Loss to Noise Exposure*, 1954.

AMES, D. R., "Thyroid Responses to Sound Stress," *Journal of Animal Science*, 1971.

ANDERSON, GRANT S., and GOTTEMOELLER, FREDERICK, *Urban Highway Planning for Minimum Noise*, presented 138th Meeting, The American Association for the Advancement of Science, 1971.

ANDO, Y., and HATTORI, H., "Effects of Intense Noise during Fetal Life upon Postnatal Adaptability," *The Journal of the Acoustical Society of America*, April, 1970.

ANIMAL RESPONSE SUBCOMMITTEE, *An Annotated Bibliography on Animal Response to Sonic Booms and Other Loud Sounds,* National Academy of Sciences, 1970.

AREHART, L. A., and AMES, D. R., "Effects of Sound on Performance of Early-Weaned Lambs," *Journal of Animal Science,* 1970.

ARGUELLES, A. E., and MARTINEZ, M. A., in Welch & Welch, *Physiological Effects of Noise,* New York & London, Plenum Press, 1970.

ARMSTRONG, LARRY, "Voiceprints Have Won a Hearing," *Electronics,* January 17, 1972.

ARVAY, A., in Welch & Welch, *Physiological Effects of Noise,* New York & London, Plenum Press, 1970.

AYLOR, DONALD E., "How Plants and Soil Muffle Noise," *Frontiers of Plant Science,* The Connecticut Agricultural Experiment Station, Spring, 1971.

BARON, ROBERT ALEX, *Construction Noise, A Citizen's Viewpoint,* 1972 International Conference on Transportation and the Environment, Society of Automotive Engineers, N.Y., August, 1972.

——————, *The Tyranny of Noise,* New York, St. Martin's Press, 1970.

BECKER, R. W.; POZA, F.; and KRYTER, K. D., *A Study of Sensitivity to Noise,* Stanford Research Institute, 1971.

BELL, WILSON B., "Animal Response to Sonic Booms," *The Journal of the Acoustical Society of America,* September 27, 1971.

BERENEK, LEO L., "Noise," *Scientific American,* December, 1966.

BERGER, MICHAEL M., Testimony, Environmental Protection Agency public hearing, 1971.

BERLAND, THEODORE, *The Fight for Quiet,* Englewood Cliffs, N.J., Prentice-Hall, 1970.

BOETTGER, WOLFGANG A., "A Survey of Aircraft Noise Standards and Monitoring Systems at International Airport," Environmental Standards Division, Inglewood, California, July, 1972.

BOND, JAMES, and WINCHESTER, CLARENCE F., *Effects of Loud Sounds on the Physiology and Behavior of Swine,* U.S. Department of Agriculture, March, 1963.

BORSKY, PAUL, *Effects of Noise in the Community,* presented 138th meeting, American Association for the Advancement of Science, 1971.

BOTSFORD, JAMES, Panel Discussion, Environmental Protection Agency public hearing, 1971.

————, *Proposed American Standard for Community Noise*, presented 138th meeting, American Association for the Advancement of Science, 1971.

————, *Relation of Hearing Impairment to Noise Exposure and Age*, presented 83rd meeting, Acoustical Society of America, 1972.

BRAGDON, CLIFFORD R., *Community Noise Management*, presented 138th Meeting, American Association for the Advancement of Science, 1971.

BROWN, H. B. "The Horseless Carriage Means Trouble," *The New York Times*, March 25, 1973; reprinted from *Yale Law Journal*, February, 1908.

BURKHARDT, DIETRICH; SCHLEIDT, WOLFGANG; and ALTNER, HELMUT; transl. Morgan, Kenneth, *Signals in the Animal World*, London, George Allen & Unwin, Ltd., 1967.

CALLAGHAN, TOM, Testimony, Environmental Protection Agency public hearing, 1971.

CARLESTAM, GOSTA, "Noise—the Scourge of Modern Society," *Ambio*, June, 1972.

CARR, JEROME, Testimony, Environmental Protection Agency public hearing, 1971.

COHEN, ALEXANDER, ET AL., *Effects of Noise on Task Performance*, Occupational Health Research and Training Facility, January, 1966.

COHEN, ALEXANDER, *Industrial Noise and Its Effect on Hearing*, presented 138th meeting, American Association for the Advancement of Science, 1971.

————, Personal communication, November 3, 1966.

————, "Physiological and Psychological Effects of Noise on Man," *Journal of the Boston Society of Civil Engineers*, January, 1965.

COHEN, SHELDON, and SMITH, MICHAEL, *Acoustic Stimulation in Infant Rats and Adult Task Performance*, New York University Research Center for Human Relations.

COLUMBIA ENGINEERING RESEARCH, "Booms and Superbooms," June, 1972.

COOK, DAVID I., and VAN HAVERBEKE, DAVID F., *Trees and Shrubs for*

Noise Abatement, Forest Service, U.S. Department of Agriculture, and University of Nebraska College of Agriculture, July, 1971.

CUADRA, ELIZABETH; ELKINS, TERRY; and BACH, DAVID, *Noise Control by Regulation,* presented 84th Meeting of Acoustical Society of America, 1972.

CULLITON, BARBARA J., "Noise: Polluting the Environment," *Science News,* January 31, 1970.

CUMMINGS, WILLIAM C., and THOMPSON, PAUL O., "Bioacoustics of Marine Mammals," *Antarctic Journal,* September-October, 1971.

DARNER, C. L., "Sound Pulses and the Heart," *Journal of the Acoustical Society of America,* 1966.

DEAFNESS RESEARCH FOUNDATION, THE, *Progress through Research, 1958 to 1972.*

DICKERSON, DAVID O., editor-in-chief, *Transportation Noise Pollution Control and Abatement,* ASEE-NASA Langley Research Center, 1970.

DICKINSON, WILLIAM B., JR., *Noise Suppression,* Educational Research Reports, October 30, 1963.

DIEHL, GEORGE M., *Noise Control of Construction Equipment,* presented 138th meeting, American Association for the Advancement of Science, 1971.

DOUGHERTY, JOHN, Testimony, Environmental Protection Agency public hearing, 1971.

EAST CENTRAL FLORIDA REGIONAL PLANNING COUNCIL, *Cape Kennedy Regional Airport,* U.S. Department of Housing & Urban Development, 1971.

EPICTETUS, *Fragments VI,* translated by E. Carter.

ETTER, DR. ALFRED, *Noise the Ultimate Insult,* testimony, Environmental Protection Agency, 1971.

EYRING, CARL F., "Jungle Acoustics," *The Journal of the Acoustical Society of America,* October, 1946.

FALK, STEPHEN A., "Combined Effects of Noise and Ototoxic Drugs," *Environmental Health Perspectives,* October, 1972.

FAY, THOMAS H., JR., ET AL., "Audiologic and Otologic Screening of

Disadvantaged Children," *Archives of Otolaryngology,* April, 1970.

FEDERAL AVIATION ADMINISTRATION, *Aircraft Noise Abatement Program, 1971–1972.*

—————, *Civil Airplane Noise Reduction Retrofit Requirements, Advance Notice of Proposed Rule Making,* Federal Register, November 4, 1970.

—————, *Noise Type Certification and Acoustical Change Approvals, Notice of Proposed Rule Making,* Federal Register, September 17, 1971.

—————, *Part 36—Noise Standards: Aircraft Type Certification,* Federal Register, November 18, 1969.

—————, *Civil Aircraft Sonic Boom, Notice of Proposed Rule Making,* Federal Register, April 16, 1970.

—————, *Civil Supersonic Aircraft Noise Type Certification Standards,* Federal Register, August 6, 1970.

FIDELL, SANFORD, Panel Discussion, Environmental Protection Agency public hearing, 1971.

FINKELMAN, JAY, and GLASS, DAVID C., "Reappraisal of the Relationship between Noise and Human Performance by means of a Subsidiary Task Measure," *Journal of Applied Psychology,* 1970.

FORSTER, FRANCIS M., "Epileptic Seizures Induced by Sound," in Welch & Welch, *Physiological Effects of Noise,* 1970.

FOWLER, EDMUND P., JR., and FAY, THOMAS H., JR., "Hearing Impairment in a Medical Center Population," *Archives of Otolaryngology,* March, 1961.

FOX, MEYER S., *Indiana Medical Journal,* 1970.

GATLEY, WILLIAM S., and FRYE, EDWIN E., "Regulation of Noise in Urban Areas," *A Manual Prepared for Workshops,* August, 1971.

GEBER, WILLIAM F., in Welch & Welch, *Physiological Effects of Noise,* 1970.

GJESDAL, FINN, "Panic Injuries in Fur Farms," *Nord. Vet.-Med.,* 1963.

GLASS, DAVID C., ET AL., *Perceived Control of Aversive Stimulation and the Reduction of Stress Responses,* 1972.

GLASS, DAVID C.; REIM, BRUCE; and SINGER, JEROME E., "Behavioral Consequences of Adaptation to Controllable and Uncontrollable Noise," *Journal of Experimental Social Psychology,* March, 1971.

GLASS, DAVID C., and SINGER, JEROME E., *Behavioral Aftereffects of Un-*

predictable and Uncontrollable Noise, presented 138th meeting, American Association for the Advancement of Science, 1971.

GLASS, DAVID C.; SINGER, JEROME E.; and FRIEDMAN, LUCY N., "Psychic Cost of Adaptation to an Environmental Stressor," *Journal of Personality and Social Psychology,* 1969.

GLORIG, ARAM, *Hearing Conservation in Industry,* Maico Audiological Library Series.

GREENWALD, ALVIN G., "Law of Noise Pollution," *Environment Reporter,* May 1, 1970.

GRENELL, ROBERT G., *Brain Mechanisms and High Level Ambient Noise,* presented Environmental Protection Agency public hearing, 1971.

GRIMALDI, JOHN V., "Noise and Human Safety," *National Safety Council News,* February, 1957.

HALSTEAD, HARRISON, "Stratospheric Ozone with Added Water Vapor: Influence of High-Altitude Craft," *Science,* November 13, 1970.

HALSTEAD, W. C., *ONR Benox Report,* 1953.

HANNAH, HAROLD W., "Loss of Animals by Fright," *Journal of the American Veterinary Medical Association,* October 15, 1969.

HARRIS, CYRIL M., ed., *Handbook of Noise Control,* New York, McGraw-Hill Book Co., 1957.

HARRIS, CYRIL M., and ROSENTHAL, ALBERT J., *Memorandum re New York City Noise Control Code,* March 13, 1972.

HARRISON, ROBIN, *Motorcycle Noise,* U.S. Department of Agriculture, Forest Service, February, 1974.

—————, *Snowmobile Noise,* U.S. Department of Agriculture, Forest Service, January, 1974.

—————, Testimony, Environmental Protection Agency public hearing, 1971.

HASTEN, JACK, Testimony, Environmental Protection Agency public hearing, 1971.

HILDEBRAND, JAMES L., "Noise Pollution: An Introduction to the Problem and an Outline for Future Legal Research," *Columbia Law Review,* April, 1970.

HILLS, JASPER J. LOFTUS, and JOHNSTONE, BRIAN M., "Auditory Function, Communication, and the Brain-Evoked Response in Anuran Amphibians," *Journal of the Acoustical Society of America*, April, 1970.

HIRABAYASHI, TIMOTHY, *Noise and the Snowmobile*, presented Purdue University, July, 1971.

HUBBARD, HARVEY H., *Generation and Control of Aircraft Noise and Sonic Boom*, presented 138th meeting, American Association for the Advancement of Science, 1971.

JACKSON, ROY P., *Remarks*, NASA Lewis Research Center, Conference on Aircraft Engine Noise Reduction, 1972.

JAPAN GOVERNMENT, *Environmental Quality Standards for Noise*, Cabinet Decision, May 25, 1971. *Standards for the Control of Noises Made at Specific Factory; Noise Prevention Equipment, Safety Regulations for Road Vehicles; Factory Noise; Construction Noise; Noise Control Law of 1968*.

JAPAN MINISTRY OF HEALTH AND WELFARE, *White Paper on Pollution*, 1970.

JENSEN, MARCUS M., "Audiogenic Stress and Susceptibility to Infection," Welch & Welch, *Physiological Effects of Noise*, New York & London, Plenum Press, 1970.

JERISON, HARRY J., "Performance on a Simple Vigilance Task in Noise and Quiet," *The Journal of the Acoustical Society of America*, November, 1957.

JET AIRCRAFT NOISE PANEL, *Alleviation of Jet Aircraft Noise Near Airports*, Office of Science and Technology, March, 1966.

JOINER, J. W., Testimony, Environmental Protection Agency public hearing, 1971.

JONES, GLENN, Testimony, Environmental Protection Agency public hearing, 1971.

KAHL, M. PHILIP, "The Courtship of Storks," *Natural History*, October, 1972.

KAUFMAN, JAMES J., *Legal Aspects of Noise*, presented 138th meeting, American Association for the Advancement of Science, 1971.

KODAMA, HABUKU, *Psychological Effect of Aircraft Noise upon Inhabitants of an Airport Neighborhood*, presented 17th International Congress of Applied Psychology, Liège, Belgium, July, 1971.

KOLK, FRANKLIN, Testimony, Environmental Protection Agency public hearing, 1971.

KRYTER, KARL D., *The Effects of Noise on Man,* New York & London, Academic Press, 1970.

————, chairman, *Non-Auditory Effects of Noise,* Report of Working Group 63, NAS-NRC Committee on Hearing, Bioacoustics, and Biomechanics, 1971.

LANG, WILLIAM W., *Product Noise and Its Control,* presented 138th meeting, American Association for the Advancement of Science, 1971.

LEMPERT, BARRY L., and HENDERSON, T. L., *Occupational Noise and Hearing, 1968 to 1972,* National Institute for Occupational Safety and Health, Cincinnati, Ohio, 1973.

LEWIN, STUART F., "Noise Pollution," *Law and the Municipal Ecology,* National Institute of Municipal Law Officers, 1970.

LEWIS RESEARCH CENTER, *Aircraft Engine Noise Reduction,* a conference, 1972.

LINDSAY, DR. JOHN R., Personal Communication, January 24, 1972.

LIPSCOMB, DAVID M., *Noise in the Environment: The Problem; Recreational and Environmental Sounds,* Maico Audiological Library Series, 1969.

————, *Report to Legislative Council Committee, State of Tennessee,* 1970.

LOCKETT, MARY F., "Effects of Sound on Endocrine Function," in Welch & Welch, *Physiological Effects of Noise,* 1970.

LUKAS, JEROME S., *Awakening Effects of Simulated Sonic Booms and Aircraft Noise on Men and Women,* presented Symposium on Sonic Boom Exposure Effects, Saltsjobaden, Sweden, September 7–9, 1971.

————, Personal Communication, January 20, 1972.

LUKAS, JEROME S.; DOBBS, MARY E.; and KRYTER, KARL D., *Disturbance of Human Sleep by Subsonic Jet Aircraft Noise and Simulated Sonic Booms,* Stanford Research Institute, July, 1971.

LUKAS, JEROME S., and KRYTER, KARL D., "Awakening Effects of Simulated Sonic Booms and Subsonic Aircraft Noise," in Welch & Welch, *Physiological Effects of Noise,* New York & London, Plenum Press, 1971.

LYNCH, CHARLES J., "Noise Control," *International Science and Technology,* April, 1966.

MCCARTHY, DESMOND C., "Restrictions on Noise Emitted by Motorized Vehicles," Testimony, Environmental Protection Agency public hearing, 1971.

MACLEAN, WILLIAM R., "On the Acoustics of Cocktail Parties," *The Journal of the Acoustical Society of America,* January, 1959.

MAAS, R. B., *How to Comply with the U.S. Labor Department's Occupational Safety and Health Act Rules and Regulations Pertaining to Noise,* Maico Audiological Library Series, 1971.

MAJEAU-CHARGOIS, DEBORAH A.; BERLIN, CHARLES I.; and WHITEHOUSE, GERALD D., "Sonic Boom Effects on the Organ of Corti," *Laryngoscope,* April, 1970.

MEASURES, MARY, and WEINBERGER, PEARL, "The Effect of Four Audible Sound Frequencies on the Growth of Marquis Spring Wheat," *Canadian Journal of Botany,* 1970.

MECKLIN, JOHN M., "It's Time to Turn Down All That Noise," *Fortune,* October 30, 1969.

MEYER, ALVIN, chairman, Discussion, Environmental Protection Agency public hearing, 1971.

MILLER, LAYMON N., *Human Response to Noise,* presented 138th meeting, American Association for the Advancement of Science, 1971.

MINEKELY, B. B., *Nursing Research,* 1968.

NAHB RESEARCH FOUNDATION, *Acoustical Manual, Apartment and Home Construction,* June, 1971.

NATIONAL CENTER FOR HEALTH STATISTICS, *Health in the Later Years of Life,* October, 1971.

NATIONAL CLEARINGHOUSE FOR MENTAL HEALTH INFORMATION, *Pollution, Its Impact on Mental Health,* 1972.

NATIONAL INDUSTRIAL POLLUTION CONTROL COUNCIL, *Report,* May, 1971.

NATIONAL INSTITUTE FOR OCCUPATIONAL SAFETY AND HEALTH, *Crite-*

ria for a Recommended Standard . . . Occupational Exposure to Noise,
U.S. Department of Health, Education, and Welfare, 1972.

NATIONAL RESEARCH COUNCIL OF CANADA, *Snowmobile Noise, Its Sources, Hazards and Control,* 1970.

NEHER, G. M., project director, *The Role of Noise as a Physiological Stressor,* Environmental Control Administration, August, 1970.

NEW YORK CITY ENVIRONMENTAL PROTECTION ADMINISTRATION, *Airport and Aircraft Noise in New York City,* October, 1973.

——————, *Rapid Transit Railroad Noise,* October, 1973.

New York City Noise Control Code, 1972.

Noise Control Act of 1972, Public Law 92–574, 92nd Congress, H.R. 11021, October 27, 1972.

NOONE, JAMES A., *Environment Report, National Journal,* October 14, 1972.

NORWOOD, MALCOLM, *The World of Deafness—as Viewed by an Insider,* presented 83rd meeting, Acoustical Society of America, 1972.

Occupational Safety and Health Act of 1970, *Federal Register,* May 29, 1971.

ODA, RYOSUKE, "Influence of Noise on the Activities of Dairy Cattle and Laying Hens," *Bulletin of the Faculty of Agriculture, Yamaguti University,* Japan, 1959.

OFFICE OF SCIENCE & TECHNOLOGY, *Alleviation of Jet Aircraft Noise near Airports,* March, 1966.

ORGANIZATION FOR ECONOMIC CO-OPERATION AND DEVELOPMENT, *Urban Traffic Noise,* Paris, 1971.

ORLOFF, NEIL, *The Environmental Impact Statement Process,* presented Environmental Impact Statement Seminar, Twin Cities Federal Executive Board, Minneapolis, February 6, 1973.

OSAKA MUNICIPAL GOVERNMENT, *Environmental Pollution in Osaka City,* 1971.

OSTERGAARD, PAUL B., *Can Industrial Plants Be Adequately Quieted?,* presented 138th meeting, American Association for the Advancement of Science, 1971

OSTWALD, PETER F. *Psychiatric Considerations of the Noise Problem.*

190 *Bibliography*

PITARO, REV. MSGR. MIMIE B., Testimony, Environmental Protection Agency public hearing, 1971.

POLLACK, IRWIN, and PICKETT, J. M., "Cocktail Party Effect," *The Journal of the Acoustical Society of America,* November, 1957.

PONOMARENKO, I., *Hygiene and Sanitation,* 1966.

POWERS, JOHN O., *The Federal Aviation Administration's Environmental Activities,* prepared for Bay Area Air Transportation Conference, 1971.

—————, *Jet Engine Noise Data from Subsonic Aircraft,* prepared for International Short Course on Aircraft Noise Theory and Application, 1971.

PROSEK, JOHN, Testimony, Environmental Protection Agency public hearing, 1971.

QUIET HIGHWAYS COUNCIL, INC., THE, *Statement of Purpose,* 1972.

REID, KENNETH H., "Periodical Cicada: Mechanism of Sound Production," *Science,* May 28, 1971.

REIM, BRUCE; GLASS, DAVID C.; and SINGER, JEROME E., "Behavioral Consequences of Exposure to Uncontrollable and Unpredictable Noise," *Journal of Applied Social Psychology,* 1971.

Report of the Mayor's Task Force on Noise Control, A, *Toward a Quieter City,* January, 1970.

Report of the Panel on Noise Abatement, *The Noise Around Us,* U.S. Department of Commerce, September, 1970.

RETALLACK, DOROTHY, *The Sound of Music and Plants,* Santa Monica, California, DeVorss & Co., 1973.

RICE, BERKELEY, "The Snowmobile Is an American Dream Machine," *New York Times Magazine,* February 13, 1972.

RINGHAM, R. F., Testimony, Environmental Protection Agency public hearing, 1971.

ROBINSON, B. WHEELER, Comment, *The Journal of the Acoustical Society of America,* 1961.

RODDA, MICHAEL, *Noise and Society,* London, Oliver & Boyd, Ltd., 1967.

ROSEN, SAMUEL, in Welch & Welch, *Physiological Effects of Noise,* New York & London, Plenum Press, 1970.

ROYAL MINISTRY FOR FOREIGN AFFAIRS, ROYAL MINISTRY OF AGRICUL-
TURE, *The Nordic Environmental Protection Convention with a Com-
mentary,* Stockholm, Sweden, February 19, 1974.

RUDDLESDEN, F., *Some Observations on the Effect of Bang Type Noises on
Laying Birds,* Royal Aircraft Establishment, April, 1971.

SACKLER, ARTHUR M., and WELTMAN, A. STANLEY, *Behavioral and Endocrine Effects of Noise Stimuli on Normal and Seizure Susceptible Rats,*
presented Environmental Protection Agency public hearing, 1971.

SCHIFLETT, SAM, Personal Communication, February 9, 1972.

SCHMID, CHARLES, Testimony, Environmental Protection Agency public
hearing, 1971.

SCHULTZ, THEODORE J., *Community Noise Ordinances in the United
States and Europe,* presented 138th meeting, American Association for
the Advancement of Science, 1971.

SCHULTZ, THEODORE J., and MCMAHON, NANCY M., *Noise Assessment
Guidelines,* U.S. Department of Housing and Urban Development, August, 1971.

SCOTT, WILLIAM N., *Vehicular Noise,* presented 138th meeting American
Association for the Advancement of Science, 1971.

SEBEOK, THOMAS A., ed., *Animal Communication,* Indiana University
Press, 1968.

SETTERS, WELDON, "Adaptation and Fatigue;" *The Journal of the Acoustical Society of America,* November, 1964.

SHATOLOV, N. N., ET AL., *Russian Laboratory Hygiene and Occupational
Diseases,* 1962.

SHURCLIFF, WILLIAM A., *SST Handbook for 1972,* Citizens League
Against the Sonic Boom.

SIDDON, THOMAS E., *Jet Noise Research—Progress and Prognosis,* presented Inter-Noise 72 Proceedings, 1972.

SIERRA CLUB-ANGELES CHAPTER, *Summary of Activities,* 1972.

SIRIANNI, REPRESENTATIVE RALPH E., Testimony, Environmental Protection Agency, public hearing, 1971.

SOCIETY FOR THE SUPPRESSION OF UNNECESSARY NOISE, New York, 1907.

SONTAG, LESTER, W., "Effect of Noise during Pregnancy upon Fetal and
Subsequent Adult Behavior," in Welch & Welch, *Physiological Effects*

of Noise, New York & London, Plenum Press, 1970.

————, "Prenatal Determinants of Postnatal Behavior," in Waisman and Kerr, eds., *Fetal Growth and Development,* New York, McGraw-Hill, 1970.

SPARKS, CECIL R., Testimony, Environmental Protection Agency public hearing, 1971.

SPERRY, WILLIAM C., *The Federal Aviation Administration Aircraft Noise Abatement Program, FY–71–72,* prepared for Seminar on Noise Pollution of the Urban Environment, University of Wisconsin Institute, 1970.

STANDLEY, DAVID, Testimony, Environmental Protection Agency public hearing, 1971.

SWART, BERNIE, "Truck Noise Control," *Fleet Owner,* January, 1963.

TAMARI, I., "Reproductive Function and Audiogenic Stimuli," in Welch & Welch, *Physiological Effects of Noise,* New York & London, Plenum Press, 1970.

THIESSEN, GEORGE J., "Effects of Noise During Sleep," in Welch & Welch, *Physiological Effects of Noise,* 1970.

TOKYO METROPOLITAN GOVERNMENT, *An Administrative Perspective of Tokyo,* March, 1972.

————, *Tokyo Fights Pollution,* March, 1971.

————, *Tokyo's Housing Problem,* March, 1972.

TOKYO METROPOLITAN RESEARCH INSTITUTE, *The Tokyo Metropolitan Environmental Pollution Control Ordinance and its Enforcement Regulation,* July, 1971.

TRACOR, *Community Reaction to Airport Noise,* National Aeronautics and Space Administration, July, 1971.

TRAVIS, HUGH F., ET AL., *An Interdisciplinary Study of the Effects of Real and Simulated Sonic Booms on Farm-Raised Mink,* U.S. Department of Agriculture, August, 1972.

UNITED NATIONS, "Tallinin," *UNESCO Features,* June, 1971.

U.S. DEPARTMENT OF HOUSING AND URBAN DEVELOPMENT, *Circular, Noise Abatement and Control: Departmental Policy,* August 4, 1971.

U.S. ENVIRONMENTAL PROTECTION AGENCY, *EPA Citizens' Bulletins,* 1973.

—————, *Information on Levels of Environmental Noise Requisite to Protect Public Health and Welfare with an Adequate Margin of Safety*, March, 1974.

—————, "Noise and Transportation," *EPA Bulletin*, January, 1972.

—————, *Environmental News*, 1973.

—————, *EPA's Noise Abatement Program*, presented 2nd National Meeting of National Organization to Insure a Sound-Controlled Environment, 1971.

—————, *Noise Workshop of the National Symposium on State Environmental Legislation*, 1972.

—————, *President's 1971 Environmental Program, The*, 1971.

—————, *Report to the President and Congress on Noise*, December 31, 1971.

—————, *Report on Aircraft-Airport Noise*, August, 1973.

VON GIERKE, HENNING, Panel Discussion, Evironmental Protection Agency public hearing, 1971.

WARD, W. DIXON, "The Concept of Susceptibility to Hearing Loss," *Journal of Occupational Medicine*, December, 1965.

—————, "Temporary Threshold Shift in Males and Females," *The Journal of the Acoustical Society of America*, August, 1966.

—————, Testimony, Environmental Protection Agency public hearing, 1971.

WATERS, JOHN F.: MCFADDEN, JOHN V.; and GLASS, RAY E., *Aircraft Noise Type Certification Orientation Session*, Hydrospace Research Corporation, October, 1970.

WEINBERGER, PEARL, and MEASURES, MARY, "The Effect of Two Audible Sound Frequencies on the Germination and Growth of a Spring and Winter Wheat," *Canadian Journal of Botany*, 1968.

WELCH, BRUCE L., Testimony, Environmental Protection Agency public hearing, 1971.

WELCH, BRUCE L., and WELCH, ANNEMARIE S., editors, *Physiological Effects of Noise*, New York & London, Plenum Press, 1970.

WHITCOMB, MILTON, Panel Discussion, Environmental Protection Agency public hearing, 1971.

194   *Bibliography*

WILLIAMS, HAROLD L., "Effects of Noise during Sleep," in Welch & Welch, *Physiological Effects of Noise,* New York & London, Plenum Press, 1970.

WINZER, GEORGE E., *Design of Noise Control in Housing,* presented, 138th meeting, American Association for the Advancement of Science, 1971.

YAFFE, CHARLES D., and JONES, HERBERT H., *Noise and Hearing,* U.S. Public Health Service, 1961.

YEAKEL, E. H., ET AL., *American Journal of Physiology,* 1948.

YOST, NICHOLAS C., *Statement Before Hearing Conducted by the Aviation Subcommittee,* U.S. Senate Commerce Committee, Inglewood, California, March 30, 1973.

ZARCONE, V., ET AL., from *Archives of General Psychology,* 1968.

Periodicals

The large number of newspapers, magazines and technical journals consulted include:

Abstracts, Acoustical Society of America
Aviation Daily
Aviation Week and Space Technology
Business Week
Chicago Tribune
Christian Science Monitor
Daily Times (Mamaroneck, N.Y.)
Dun's Review
Hearing and Speech News
Journal of the Acoustical Society of America
Mainichi Daily News (Japan)
Medical Tribune
Nature
New Scientist (Britain)
New York Times
Newsweek
Noise/News

Quiet, Citizens for a Quieter City
Science Dimensions (Canada)
Sound and Vibration
Time
U.S. News and World Report
Washington Post

INDEX

INDEX

Acoustical material. *See* soundproofing
"Acoustical perfume." *See* White noise
Acoustical Society of America, 37, 51, 157
Acoustics, 116, 117, 137
Adaptation. *See* Noise, adjustment to
Advertising Age, 172
Air compressor, 4, 22, 76, 88, 90, 98, 120–21, 171, 176
Air conditioning, 25, 111–12, 114–15, 117, 125, 130, 139
Airplane, 4–5, 9–11, 14–15, 20–23, 28–39, 32, 37–39, 41, 43–44, 56, 62–69, 71, 76, 84–86, 93, 103–6, 110, 116, 122–23, 144–65, 168, 171–73, 176–77
Airplane, supersonic. *See* Supersonic airplane
Airport, 10, 12, 21, 23, 28, 32, 35, 68–69, 77, 80, 94, 96, 103–6, 122–23, 125, 127, 130, 144–50, 153–54, 158, 160–61, 163–65, 169–70
Airport Land Use Commission, 148
All American Airways, 145
Alpheidae, 72
American Airlines, 159
American Association for the Advancement of Science, 89, 111

American Society of Engineering Education, 19
Ando, Dr. Y., 32
Anesthesia, noise, 27–28
Animals, effects of noise, 1, 4, 12, 16, 32–35, 48–50, 54–55, 57–74, 176
Animals, laboratory, 32–34, 48–50, 55, 57, 58–62
Anti-Concorde Project, 153
Anti-noise, 117–18
Anti-Noise League, 137
Anxiety, 11, 15, 21, 30–31, 106
Appliances, 111–17, 126, 139, 171
Arai, Kazuo, 97
Association for Living Pollution Control, 108
Association of American Scientists, 152
Association of Victims of Noise Pollution, 107
Audiometer test, 38, 41, 45, 48, 163, 171
Automobile, 13, 49, 54, 76, 82, 87–90, 94, 102–3, 130–39, 141–42, 144, 168, 171–73, 175–77
Aylor, Dr. Donald E., 141

Baba, Mieko, 107

Balloon, 164
Barnes Junior High School, 9
Baron, Robert Alex, 170–71
Barrier, 116, 133, 142–43, 168, 174
Bat, 1–2, 70, 73
Behavior, irrational, 7–10, 13
Bell, Alexander Graham, 5
Bell, Wilson B., 63
Berland, Theodore, 171
Bermuda, 137
Bird, 1, 5, 25, 36, 54, 69–74, 119, 175, 177
Boeing airplanes, 159–60, 162
Boeing Company, 152, 160–61
Bogard, Dr. Howard M., 15, 21
"Boilermakers' disease," 78
Bolt, Berenek and Newman, 89, 127, 136, 150, 168
Bond, Dr. James, 63, 65
Borsky, Dr. Paul, 28, 42, 149
Botsford, Dr. James, 46
Bowman, Professor Robert E., 13
British Symposium on Control of Noise, 47
Broadbent, Dr. Donald E., 18–19, 24
Brown, Justice H. B., 134, 172
Building code, 77, 99, 124, 171
Burglar alarm, 88–89
Bus, 9, 102, 173, 177
By Our Own Hands, 107–8

Cage, John, 52
California, University of, 58–59
Callaghan, Tom, 145, 149
Canyon de Chelly, 151, 155
Cap pistol, 49–50
Cape Kennedy Regional Airport, 68–69
Caterpillar Tractor Company, 119
Cattle, 63–64, 66
Children, effects of noise, 9, 14, 21, 48–50, 53, 105–6
Cholesterol, 57
Citizens' action, 72, 103, 105, 107–9, 144, 153, 163–65, 167–73, 176–77
Citizens Against Noise, 171
Citizens for a Quieter City, 119, 170–71
Citizens League Against the Sonic Boom, 72, 150

City, 2, 6, 9–10, 25, 37, 51, 54, 56–57, 85, 88, 93–95, 99, 110–11, 133, 136, 171–75
Close, William H., 133
Clean Air Act Amendments, 84
Cocktail parties, 51–52
Cohen, Alexander, 42
Cohen, Sheldon, 33
Columbia University, 18, 28, 42, 79, 125, 138, 149, 174
Committee to Save Our Serenity, 165
Common Cause, 152
Concentration in noise, 22, 25–27, 62
Concorde, 65, 153–56
Connecticut Agricultural Experiment Station, 141
Construction, 4, 8, 10, 21–22, 41, 44, 49, 56, 66, 76, 84, 88, 90–91, 93–94, 98–99, 107, 116, 118–21, 124–27, 129–30, 164, 171, 174, 176
Conversation, 9, 20, 25, 36, 46, 51–52, 56, 85, 93, 96, 112, 119, 126, 128, 160
Cook, Dr. David I., 140
Corti, organ of, 36, 40, 48, 50
Cotton, 47
Countryside, 1–2, 6, 85, 88, 140, 162, 175
Crazy Horse Saloon, 6
Cummings, Dr. William C., 71–72
Curfew, 87–88, 104, 119, 145–46, 149–50, 172, 177
Cycles per second. See frequency

Danto, Dr. Joseph, 43
Deafness. See Hearing
Deafness Research Foundation, 37
Death, 11, 59, 61, 65–66, 156
Decibel, 5, 6, 11–14, 19, 26–28, 33, 38, 40–46, 48, 50–52, 54, 57–59, 61, 67, 72, 79–80, 85, 87–88, 91, 93, 96, 105, 110–12, 117, 119–20, 122–23, 126–27, 130, 132–33, 135–36, 138–39, 144, 149, 152, 159–60, 162, 164–65, 167, 174
Decibel, definition, 5
Decibel scales, 19
Deutsch, C. P., 33–34
Diehl, George M., 120–21
Discotheque, 5, 50, 67
Dog, 3, 11, 19–20, 60, 66, 119
Dream, 15–16

Drexel University, 133
Drugs, 9, 17, 51
Drugs, ototoxic, 48–49
Dubos, Dr. René, 110

Ear, 5, 31, 36, 38–41, 44–45, 47–49, 62, 73, 75, 106, 118, 133
Ear protectors, 24, 43, 46–47, 80, 91, 171
Earthworm, 1
Echolocation, 1–2, 72–73
Ecology, 3–4, 68, 69, 70–71, 73–74, 76, 83
Efficiency, 12, 16, 24–25, 96, 114
Energy crisis, 86, 133, 170
Engine, 3–4, 42, 58, 84, 118–19, 131–33, 138, 142, 152–53, 155, 159–61, 163–64
Environment, 3–4, 20, 33, 39, 102, 109, 111, 152–53, 168, 175–76. See also Ecology
Environmental Defense Fund, 152
Environmental impact statement, 83–84, 147, 169
Epictetus, 36, 51
Epilepsy, 60
Eskimo, 3
Eye, 58

Falk, Dr. Stephen A., 48–49
Farm, 2–3, 61, 63–67, 76, 85, 110, 140, 176
Farr, Dr. Lee E., 112
Fatigue, 13, 16, 24, 27, 42, 55–56, 58, 112
Fear, 6, 23, 54–56, 62, 66, 69, 70–71, 176
Federal Aviation Administration. See U.S. Department of Transportation, Federal Aviation Administration
Federal Aviation Regulation. See Part 36
Fenelon castle, 156
Fetus, effects of noise, 29–33, 105
Fields, W. C., 17
Fines, 87–89, 98, 102, 120, 137
Fleet Owner, 83
Fletcher, Professor John L., 70, 71, 73–74
Flight procedures, 41, 105, 145–50, 162–63, 177
Fox, 64, 68–69, 176
Franklin, Benjamin, 176
French, John III, 168
Frequency, 1, 6, 19, 27, 37–42, 46, 48–49, 70–74, 78, 80, 117–18, 129, 141, 162, 164

Friends of the Earth, 152
Frog, 1, 54

Garbage truck, 13, 87–88, 118
General Electric Company, 160
General Motors Corp., 139
Gjesdal, Finn, 64, 70
Glass, Dr. David C., 21–23
Goodfriend, Lewis S., 25, 111, 114, 117, 121, 160
Grand Canyon, 110
Grass, 139
Greenwald, Alvin G., 124
Grenell, Dr. Robert G., 27
Griggs case, 145–46
Guitar, electric, 14, 44, 176

Hannah, Harold W., 66
Harris, Dr. Cyril M., 18, 79, 125, 129, 138, 174
Hartzog, George H., 152
Hasten, Jack, 119
Hattori, H., 32
Health, 53, 56–60, 85–86, 89, 105–6, 177
Hearing, 2, 18, 24, 36–53, 56, 59, 61–62, 70, 78–80, 85–86, 112, 133, 163, 171, 176
Hearing test. See Audiometer test
Heart disease, 56–57, 60
Heathrow Airport, 11, 20
Hebrew University, 34
Helicopter, 13, 43–44, 62, 164–65
Helplessness, 21
Helwig, Christine K., 138, 167–68
Hertz. See Frequency
Hertz, Heinrich, 37
Hibernators, 3, 73–74
Highway, 3–4, 23, 44, 80, 86, 91, 94, 96, 107, 111, 122, 126–27, 130–31, 133, 135–36, 138–42, 167–68, 170, 173–77
Hildebrand, James L., 126
Holloman Air Force Base, 16
Home decoration, 128–29
Homicide, 7–8, 13, 110
Hormones, 11, 31, 35, 54, 61–62
Horn-blowing, 13, 42–43, 54, 83, 88–91, 103, 120, 134, 137, 171, 177
Horse, 66, 131–32, 172
Hospital, 17, 49, 85, 93, 97, 125, 129, 174–75

Hot rod, 103, 137
Housing, 20–21, 77, 83, 85, 90–95, 99–100, 104, 110–11, 119, 122–30, 132–33, 138–40, 142–44, 146–48, 150, 158, 160, 162–63, 167–68, 172, 174–75, 177
Hudson River Valley Council, 169
Hypersonic airplane, 155
Hypertension, 56–58, 60–61

Icarus, 158
Illness, 15, 17, 35, 37, 53, 58–59, 106, 176
Industrial Welfare Society, 47
Industry, 12–13, 24, 26, 38–40, 43–49, 57–60, 76–81, 83, 85–87, 90–95, 99–103, 106–7, 111, 116–17, 165, 175–77
Infrasound, 38, 58
Ingersoll-Rand Company, 120
Insect, 70, 73
Institute of Environmental Quality, 87
International agreement, 175–77
Ishino, Kutaro, 104
Itami International Airport, 10, 103–5, 150
Izvestia, 91

Jackhammer, 4, 8, 41, 44, 56
Japan, 10, 32, 63–64, 92–109, 173
Jet aircraft. *See* Airplane
Job performance in noise, 16, 22–24, 26–27, 33
Jones v. *Powell,* 81, 166
Journal of Annamalai University, 75
Jungle, 54, 139
Juvenal, 7

Kennedy International Airport, 10, 125, 146, 149, 154
Knights Hospitalers of St. John of Jerusalem, 17
Koch, Robert, 177
Kodaras, Michael J., 125
Kolk, Franklin, 122, 159

Lancet, 45
Land use, 94, 100–101, 104–5, 122–26, 147–48, 162
Lang, Dr. William W., 111, 117

Law enforcement, 82–83, 87, 89–92, 97–100, 102–4, 119–20, 123, 135–37, 145, 147, 150, 166
Laws against noise, 3, 38, 43, 46, 51, 60, 77–94, 96–107, 119, 121, 124–25, 132, 134–37, 145–47, 152–54, 159–63, 166, 168–73, 176–77
Laws against noise, California, 82, 123, 126, 134–35, 146, 148
Laws against noise, Calif., Burbank, 145, 150
Laws against noise, France, 137
Laws against noise, Germany, 124, 136
Laws against noise, Ill., Chicago, 87–90
Laws against noise, Japan, 92–94, 96–107, 150
Laws against noise, Massachusetts, 135
Laws against noise, Netherlands, 124, 136–37, 172
Laws against noise, New Jersey, 87–89
Laws against noise, New York, 89, 134–35, 168
Laws against noise, N.Y., Cedarhurst, 145
Laws against noise, N.Y., Hempstead, 145, 169
Laws against noise, N.Y., New York City, 88–89, 132, 137–38, 166
Laws against noise, Rhode Island, 177
Laws against noise, South Africa, 136
Laws against noise, Sweden, 124, 136, 153
Laws against noise, Switzerland, 137, 153
Laws against noise, U.K., 81, 90–91, 124, 136, 166
Laws against noise, U.S.S.R., 58, 91, 124
Laws against noise, Vermont, 135
Lawsuits, 65–67, 78–79, 81–82, 85, 89, 105–6, 119, 123, 126, 145–46, 151, 156, 167, 169, 175–76
Learning, 26, 33–34, 89, 106
Le Bourget Airport, 150, 162
Lewin, Stuart F., 81–82
Lipscomb, Dr. David M., 38–39, 50, 151
Logan Airport, 23, 149, 154
Lombard effect, 51
Los Angeles International Airport, 123, 146–48
Los Angeles International Airport governors, 146
Lukas. Dr. Jerome S., 14, 16
Lynch, Charles J., 117

Mabaan tribe, 48, 56–57, 59–60
McDonnell Douglas airplanes, 159–60
MacLean, William R., 52
Major Appliance Consumer Action Panel, 115
Manhattan House of Detention, 9
Mass transit, 172–74, 176
Massachusetts Port Authority, 145
Matsui, Saburo, 104
Measures, Mary, 74
Medical Journal of Australia, 35
Memory, 12
Memphis, 82–83, 135–36
Mental health, 8–17, 21, 24, 26, 30–32, 35, 105–6, 110, 112, 176–77
Mental illness, 7–13, 15, 47, 64
Mesa Verde, 152, 154
Metropolitan Transportation Authority, 89, 170
Meyer, Alvin V., Jr., 84, 151
Migration, 68
Mink, 65–66
Minnesota Livestock Sanitary Board, 66
Mitkof Island, 65
Mochizuki, Tomio, 98–99
Monkey, 4, 13, 16, 61–62, 72
"Monsieur Silence," 137
Motor. *See* Engine
Motorcycle, 27, 39, 49, 73, 85, 103, 137
Mount Rainier, 3
Muffler, 87, 90, 94, 103, 117, 119, 121, 132–35, 137, 165, 168, 171, 177
Music, 4–6, 25, 30–31, 36–37, 50–52, 63, 79, 81–82, 88, 94, 106, 112, 118, 167. *See also* Rock music
Muskie, Edmund S., 86

Nakamura, Takakazu, 102, 106
Nakasuji, Noboru, 100–101
National Academy of Sciences, 10, 55, 62
National Aeronautics and Space Administration, 19, 154–55, 157, 160, 164
National Association of Home Builders, 126, 130
National Environmental Policy Act, 83–84
National Institute of Municipal Law Officers, 81–82

National Institute for Occupational Safety and Health. *See* U.S. Department of Health, Education, and Welfare
Nestle v. City of Santa Monica, 146
Neurosis. *See* Mental health, Mental illness
N.Y.C. Board of Correction, 9
N.Y.C. Bureau of Noise Abatement, 9
N.Y.C. Environmental Protection Administration, 43, 88–89
New York magazine, 126
New York University, 21, 22, 33
Newby, Dr. Hayes A., 47
Noise, adjustment to, 6, 11, 16, 32–33, 53–56, 65
Noise, annoyance, 4–5, 8, 16–20, 28, 33, 56, 81, 85–86, 89, 136–37, 142, 175–76
Noise, attitudes toward, 4–5, 19, 20–21, 23–24, 28–29, 50
Noise, complaints, 6, 8, 22–23, 28, 88–89, 91–92, 95–97, 99, 101, 105–9, 115–18, 131, 142, 149–51, 158, 163, 166–67, 169, 176
Noise, cumulative day-night average, 85, 147, 162, 174
Noise, definition, 4, 35
Noise, derivation, 35
Noise, effects of. *See* Animals, effects of noise; Children, effects of noise; Fetus, effects of noise; Sex, effects of noise; Health; Hearing; Mental health; Violence
Noise, laws. *See* Laws against noise
Noise, lawsuits. *See* Lawsuits
Noise, physiological response. *See* Physiological response to noise
Noise, psychological effects. *See* Psychological effects of noise
N.O.I.S.E., 171
Noise Abatement Society, 171–72
Noise control, cost, 97, 104, 113–15, 118–21, 130, 149, 159, 161–62
Noise Control Act, 84–87, 134, 146, 167
Noise control loans, 101, 162
Noise-control programs, industry, 24, 46–48, 78–80, 99
Noise labeling, 84, 116
Noise laboratory, 4
Noise standards, 3, 49–50, 84–88, 90, 99, 102,

109, 112, 121, 123–25, 130, 134–36, 159–61, 163, 171

Noise "thermometer," 133–34

Nord Gudvrandsdal circuit court, 64

Nordic Committee for Building Regulations, 136, 174–75

Nuisance, 81, 107, 166

Occupational Safety and Health Act, 79

Oda, Ryosuke, 63–64

Office noise, 5, 25, 118

Old age, 14, 29, 37–39, 48–50, 56, 59, 93, 135

Onishi, Shiro, 100, 102–3

Organization for Economic Cooperation and Development, 136

Orly Airport, 150, 162

Osada, Dr. Yasutaka, 106

Pain, 15, 17, 27–28, 40

Part 36, Federal Aviation Regulation, 159, 161–62

Peiper, A., 31

Penfield, Dr. Wilder, 12

Pentecostal Church of God, 158

Persich, Douglas J., 125

Personality test, 26

Physiological response to noise, 30–31, 35, 53–60, 62–64

Pickett, J. M., 51

Pig, 1, 60, 63

Pitch, 6. *See also* Frequency

Planning and Conservation League, 170

Planning council, Melbourne, Fla., 68–69

Plants, 74–76, 139–42

Plumbing, 20, 129–30

Police Anti-Noise Brigade, 137

Pollack, Irwin, 51

Pollution, air, 4–5, 9, 76, 81, 83, 96, 106–7, 131–32, 166, 172–73, 175–76

Pollution, water 4, 83, 175

Porpoise, 2, 72–73

Port Authority of N.Y. and N.J., 146, 149, 154, 169

Poultry, 66–67, 73, 88

Pravda, 154

Pregnancy, 30–34

Prehistoric cliff dwellings, 152

Preyer, W., 31

Prison, 8–9, 45–46

Privacy, 16, 20–21, 25, 129

Project to Stop the Concorde, 153

Propaganda, 28

Property damage, 146, 151, 156

Proust, Marcel, 5, 12

Psychological effects of noise, 6–13, 15–16, 21–22, 24, 26–27, 30–32, 35, 50–51, 55, 59, 63–67, 69

Quiet Highways Council, 168

Quiet Week, 171

"Quietest city," 83

Radar, 2, 27, 111

Railroad, 2, 41, 56, 60, 84, 94–98, 139, 173

Reindeer, 61

Reproduction, 34–35, 62, 64, 67, 70–71

Retallack, Dorothy, 75

Retrofit, 161–62

Rhodes, 17

Robertson, Dr. W. B., Jr., 71

Rock music, 6, 12, 44, 50–51, 56, 75–76, 90, 94, 171, 176

Romans, 7, 176

Rosen, Dr. Samuel, 48, 56

Rosenthal, Dr. Albert E., 10, 28–29, 83

Rubinstein, Artur, 5

Scandinavian convention, 175–76

Schizophrenia, 11

Schoenberner, Franz, 8

Schools, 9, 80, 85, 89, 92, 97, 104–5, 117, 123, 125–26, 175

Schopenhauer, Arthur, 34

Schultz, Dr. Theodore, 89–90, 136–37, 150

Sea, 71–72

Sex, effects of noise, 1, 12, 34–35, 63, 72–73

Shimodaira, Takashi, 102

Shooting, 8, 39, 41, 44, 49

Shurcliff, Dr. William A., 150, 152

Sierra Club, 152, 168

Sigmodon hispidus, 68–70

Simplicissimus, 8

204   *Index*

Siren, 13, 27, 42, 44, 53, 61, 76, 88, 94
Slawinski, Matthew, 78
Sleep, 6–7, 12–16, 21, 32, 96, 106, 123, 176–77
Sleep stages, 14–16
Smith, Michael, 33
Snowmobile, 3–4, 49, 73, 135
Society for the Suppression of Unnecessary Noise, 6, 17
Soil, 99, 139, 141–42
Sonar, 2, 72
Sonic boom, 14, 29, 62–63, 65–67, 71–72, 84, 151–52, 154–57
Sontag, Dr. Lester W., 30–31, 32
Soucie, G. A., 152
Sound, 1, 4–6, 25, 43–44, 61, 73–76, 97, 117–18, 127, 129, 131–32, 141–42, 148–49, 153, 155, 157, 176
Sound-level meter, 78, 80, 90, 102, 126, 135–37, 162
Sound truck, 82
Soundproofed room, 52
Soundproofing, 6, 21, 25, 97, 101, 104, 114–17, 123–30, 133, 139, 141–43, 158–63, 177
Sparks, Cecil R., 113
Speech interference. *See* Conversation
Speed, 42, 65, 72, 97, 103, 133–34, 136, 138, 140–41, 151–55, 157, 159, 168
Stanford Research Institute, 14, 16
Stockholm County Council, 148
STOLport, 163–65
Strasbourg Cathedral, 156
Striptease, 6, 175
Suburb, 4, 10, 130, 140, 174
Subway, 42–43, 44, 88–89, 96, 98, 107, 120, 125, 126, 166, 170, 173–74
Sufferers' League, 105
Suicide, 10, 13, 95–96
"Superboom," 151
Supersonic airplane, 28–29, 65, 70, 72, 150–57, 172, 177
Swiss Touring Club, 137
Sydney University, 50

Tallinin, 91
Taxi, 9, 95, 173
Technology, 2–3, 48, 85–86, 111, 113–21, 132–

33, 136, 148, 152, 154–55, 161, 164–65, 177
Temporary threshold shift, 41–45
Tennessee, University of, 4, 38, 50, 151
Thompson, Dr. Paul O., 71–72
Thruway Noise Abatement Committee, 167
Thunder, 5, 29, 61, 151
Tinnitus, 38, 48
Tires, 4, 42, 130, 133, 138–40, 167, 173, 177
Tobias, Dr. Jerry, 47
Toda, Kuniji, 104
Tokyo Metropolitan Research Institute, 95, 98–99, 111
Tosca, 37
Tourism, 28–29, 90, 109
Town-Village Noise Abatement Committee, 169
Toy, 3, 39, 40–41, 49–50, 171
TRACOR, 131
Tractor, 118–19
Traffic, 2–7, 9–10, 20, 28, 44, 49, 54, 69, 76, 93, 98, 102–3, 107, 109, 116, 124–25, 131–44, 164–65, 172–73, 176
Transportation, 83–84, 126, 172–74. *See also* Airplane, Automobile, Bus, Mass transit, Motorcycle, Railroad, Supersonic airplane, Taxi, Traffic, Truck
Tree, 2, 75, 139–42, 170
Truck, 3, 56, 84, 86, 91, 102, 130, 132–42, 167–68, 172, 177
Tufts-New England Medical Center, 125
Tunney, John V., 86–87
Tupolev-144, 153–54

Ultrasound, 2, 38, 54, 73, 75
U.S. Air Force, 28, 65–67, 155–56
U.S. Bureau of Mines, 79
U.S. Department of Agriculture, 63, 65, 140
U.S. Department of Agriculture, Forest Service, 49, 135
U.S. Department of Commerce, National Bureau of Standards, 138
U.S. Department of Health, Education, and Welfare, National Institute for Occupational Safety and Health, 42, 80
U.S. Department of Health, Education, and Welfare, Public Health Service, 46, 170

Index **205**

U.S. Department of Housing and Urban Development, 123–24, 127, 141
U.S. Department of Interior, National Park Service, 71, 152
U.S. Department of Justice, 150
U.S. Department of Transportation, 85, 132–33, 150
U.S. Department of Transportation, Federal Aviation Administration, 22, 41, 47, 84–85, 125, 144, 146–49, 152, 155, 159–61, 163–64
U.S. Environmental Protection Agency, 2, 9, 21, 23, 27, 29, 57–59, 62, 70, 77, 80, 82, 84–86, 91, 96, 110, 113, 115, 119, 122, 146–47, 161, 169, 172–73
U.S. Environmental Protection Agency, Office of Noise Abatement and Control, 83–85
U.S. Navy, 13, 72, 111
U.S. Supreme Court, 134, 145, 150, 172
Urban planning, 91, 94, 174–75

Vacuum cleaner, 112–15
Vandivert, Rod, 169–70
Van Haverbeke, Dr. David F., 140
Vibration, 96–97, 114–15, 117, 125, 176
Violence, 7–10, 13, 27, 35, 103
Von Gierke, Dr. Henning E., 155
V/STOL airplanes, 163–65

Walsh-Healey Public Contracts Act, 79–80
Ward, Dr. W. Dixon, 39
Warning, 1, 13, 23, 42, 50, 54–55, 62, 72, 121
Washing machine, 112–15
Wasp, 12
Webster, *New International Dictionary*, 35
Weinberger, Pearl, 74
Welsh, Dr. Bruce, 33, 53, 60
Whale, 71–72
White noise, 25–26, 118
White Sands Proving Grounds, 67
Wilderness, 5, 73, 176
Winzer, George E., 141
Wisconsin, University of, 112
Wisconsin Regional Primate Research Center, 13
Women, 11, 14, 39–40, 108–9
Woods Hole Oceanographic Institute, 72
World War II, 13–14, 44, 72, 95
Wright brothers, 159
Wright-Patterson Air Force Base, 26

Yeager, Capt. Charles, 157
Yost, Nicholas C., 150

Zoning, 88, 90–94, 100–102, 148, 177
Zoo, 4, 62
Zurich Polytechnic, 137